M000026200

A HISTORY OF THE

WYOMING CAPITOL

A HISTORY OF THE

WYOMING CAPITOL

STARLEY TALBOTT & LINDA GRAVES FABIAN

Foreword by Rick Ewig, Editor, *Annals of Wyoming*

THE
History
PRESS

Published by The History Press
Charleston, SC
www.historypress.com

Copyright © 2019 by Starley Talbott and Linda Graves Fabian
All rights reserved

On the back cover: The color photographs are courtesy of Michael Dixon, site architect and historic preservation consultant for the Wyoming State Capitol restoration.

First published 2019

Manufactured in the United States

ISBN 9781467141611

Library of Congress Control Number: 2019935353

Notice: The information in this book is true and complete to the best of our knowledge. It is offered without guarantee on the part of the authors or The History Press. The authors and The History Press disclaim all liability in connection with the use of this book.

All rights reserved. No part of this book may be reproduced or transmitted in any form whatsoever without prior written permission from the publisher except in the case of brief quotations embodied in critical articles and reviews.

CONTENTS

FOREWORD

The Wyoming State Capitol is more than 130 years old, and finally a comprehensive history of the state's most important building has been written. Starley Talbott and Linda Graves Fabian, in their book *A History of the Wyoming Capitol*, have provided a fascinating, entertaining and well-researched history of the capitol. The book could not be better timed, as the capitol has just been restored to its original beauty.

Talbott and Fabian begin the building's story by examining the letters of some of those involved in the construction. The territory awarded the building contract to Adam Feick & Bro., based in Sandusky, Ohio. The Feicks contracted with Robert Greenlee of Denver to oversee the construction. David Gibbs, also from Ohio, was the design architect. The Feick company sent young John Feick, Adam's son, who had never been in Wyoming, to manage the project. John's letters provide some insight into the difficulties addressed during the construction, but his letters to his wife, who stayed in Ohio, at first illustrate his difficulty adjusting to Cheyenne's weather and culture, seeing the area as perhaps a foreign land. However, eventually Feick gained respect for Wyoming, which is illustrated when he wrote "People are more liberal & a nicer class of people than you find in the east."

The authors examine two celebrations held at the capitol, one during the building's construction and the other just a few years later. The first, held on May 18, 1887, was for the laying of the capitol's cornerstone. A large crowd listened to a speech by future Wyoming governor and U.S. senator Joseph M. Carey, who spoke about Wyoming's territorial history and commented that the capitol should be "devoted to those of wisdom, good government and righteous law, which hereafter shall be enacted within it." Completed in March 1888, the capitol shortly afterward hosted the celebration of the creation of the state of Wyoming during July 1890.

President Benjamin Harrison signed Wyoming's statehood bill on July 10, 1890. Spontaneous celebrations cheering the transition to statehood occurred that day, but the official celebration was held on July 23, 1890, in Cheyenne. Nearly five thousand people enjoyed a parade and then gathered at the capitol for a series of speeches, many of which focused on the importance of Wyoming guaranteeing women full suffrage, the first state in the country to do so. The first to speak, Theresa A. Jenkins, a Wyoming suffragist, welcomed the voice of women into the national discourse. Others also spoke about that important first, and Esther Morris, whose statue stands near the capitol today, presented Governor Francis E. Warren a Wyoming flag on behalf of the new state's ladies.

Talbott and Fabian include biographical information about many Wyoming governors. These include John A. Campbell, Wyoming's first territorial governor, who on December 10, 1869, signed the bill giving women the right to vote and hold public office. Two governors who also served the state as U.S. senators are Francis E. Warren and Joseph M. Carey. Warren served twice as governor of Wyoming Territory but also as the state's first governor. Carey served as governor from 1911 to 1915, but he is noted in the book for his service as Wyoming's territorial delegate to Congress and for his efforts in writing the bill admitting Wyoming as a state and shepherding the bill through Congress. After his success in Washington, D.C., Carey returned to Cheyenne on July 26, 1890, and was welcomed by the Union Pacific band and a "surging mass" of Wyomingites who escorted him to his home and profusely thanked him for leading Wyoming to statehood. Some other governors noted are John Kendrick, Lester Hunt, Milward Simpson, Clifford Hansen, Stanley Hathaway, Ed Herschler, Mike Sullivan and Matt Mead.

Wyoming is noted for and proud of a number of firsts, many related to the role of women in the state. The authors include detailed information about Nellie Tayloe Ross, Wyoming's first woman governor and the first woman to serve as governor in the entire country. Ross ran after her husband, William Bradford Ross, who became governor in 1923, died in office. Nellie became governor in January 1925 after winning her election by more than eight thousand votes. She served two years in the office and later became the first woman to serve as director of the U.S. Mint, a position she held for twenty years. Others mentioned in the book directly related to service in the capitol are Mary Godat Bellamy, the state's first woman legislator; Verda James, the first full-term woman speaker of the state house of representatives; Harriet Elizabeth Byrd, the state's first African American woman legislator; and Estelle Reel, who was the first woman elected to statewide office in the state when she became superintendent of public instruction in 1895. Finally, Thyra Thomson is also rightly mentioned, as she was the first woman to be elected Wyoming's secretary of state, an office she held for twenty-four years.

As most know, there are prominent statues of Esther Hobart Morris and Chief Washakie at the Wyoming Capitol. Their statues also stand in Statuary Hall in the U.S. Capitol. Morris is best known as serving as the first female justice of the peace in the country, and Washakie served for many years as chief of the Shoshone tribe and is a symbol of the importance of Native Americans in the history of Wyoming. Besides the importance of these two figures standing outside the capitol, Talbott and Fabian also discuss the art featured throughout the building.

Finally, the authors describe the renovations of the Herschler Building and the capitol that have just been completed. Having the information about how the Capitol Square Project came about and how important it was to preserve and restore the capitol, which Talbott and Fabian see "as a symbol of the spirit of the people of Wyoming," is an essential part of the book.

A History of the Wyoming Capitol, by Starley Talbott and Linda Graves Fabian, is an essential and delightful telling of the history of Wyoming's capitol and many of those who served the territory and state. The building has stood since 1888, and Governor Matt Mead stated, "The restored capitol will stand for the next century—a symbol of Wyoming statehood and all it encompasses." Fortunately, our state and nation now have this engaging, well-written history of this tremendously important building to Wyoming.

—RICK EWIG

ACKNOWLEDGEMENTS

The authors wish to thank the many people who contributed to the compilation of this book. We are grateful to the early photographers who captured the construction of the original Wyoming Capitol. And we are very thankful for the many photographers and writers who have chronicled the history of this important building and its occupants.

We greatly appreciate the work of the current staff overseeing the historic renovation of the crown jewel of the capital city of Cheyenne and the state of Wyoming. We have tremendous admiration for the J.E. Dunn Construction Company (management), HDR (design and restoration management) and MOCA Systems (program management). Special thanks go to Michael Dixon, preservation architect and photographer, for information, photographs and tours. We thank Wendy Madsen, special projects manager, for a tour and insightful information. We appreciate the photographs by Rachel Girt, capital media contact, for capturing each phase of the Capitol Square Project. Our thanks also go to the many subcontractors, supervisors and a multitude of construction workers and artists who have painstakingly and lovingly spent hours and hours restoring the capitol to its historic grandeur.

Special thanks go to the staff and volunteers at the Wyoming State Archives, especially Suzi Taylor and Robin Everett. Their ability to locate materials related to the history of the capitol is remarkable.

ACKNOWLEDGEMENTS

We appreciate our acquisitions editor, Artie Crisp, our senior production editor, Mike Litchfield, and others at The History Press for their support and guidance.

Most importantly, we thank our families for their continued encouragement.

Lastly, we thank our readers and the many people who continue to inspire us with a love of history.

INTRODUCTION

The early morning light emerges across the windswept plains, moonlight wanes against a deep blue sky, and the sun glistens on the dome of the state capitol. The golden dome crowning the state house reflects the ideals of Wyoming's people.

There were few permanent settlers in Wyoming prior to the mid-1800s. Most people passed through on their way to other places. The building of the transcontinental railroad brought workers to southern Wyoming, and Cheyenne was established as a division point along the route of the railroad. General Grenville Dodge, chief engineer for the Union Pacific Railroad, selected the site because of its location at the foot of the lowest pass over the Rocky Mountains. As the workers converged on Cheyenne in 1867, they lived in tents and temporary buildings. With the hustle and bustle of those busy days, Cheyenne became famous as a "Hell on Wheels" town attracting speculators, gamblers, prostitutes and other profiteers. As the railroad construction moved on to the west, people stayed in Cheyenne and built permanent homes and businesses. The presence of the Union Pacific Railroad stabilized the economy and provided a reason for settlers to stay. Cheyenne also became a business center for the many wealthy cattle ranchers who ran their herds on the open range in southeastern Wyoming. Fort D.A. Russell, established in 1867 to protect the railroad workers from Native American attacks, also became a permanent facility in Cheyenne, now F.E. Warren Air Force Base.

Established as a territory in 1869, Wyoming quickly garnered national attention when the first territorial assembly granted all women above the age of twenty-one the right to vote. That move by the legislature made Wyoming the first territory in the United States where women were granted the voting franchise. The suffrage act was motivated by a number of factors, including enticing more women to the territory to increase the population, bringing more voters into the population and genuine concerns that women should be allowed to vote.

Wyoming was still sparsely populated in 1886, when territorial governor Francis E. Warren spoke of a need for public buildings. The territorial legislature passed a bill authorizing the construction of a capitol at a cost not to exceed $150,000. Governor Warren signed the bill on March 4, 1886, and appointed the Capitol Building Commission.

The commission purchased a site on Hill Street, now Capitol Avenue, at a cost of $13,100. David W. Gibbs of Toledo, Ohio, was selected as the architect. The company of Adam Feick & Bro. of Sandusky, Ohio, submitted the winning construction bid of $131,275.13. The contractors broke ground on September 9, 1886.

"The people should resolve that when the doors of the Capitol shall swing open to receive the officers of the territory, that he who legislates for his private gain, that he who neglects to execute and fails to honestly administer the laws, shall be driven from its portals forever," declared Joseph M. Carey, Wyoming's delegate to the U.S. Congress, at the cornerstone laying ceremony on May 18, 1887.[1]

In 1889, the Wyoming Constitutional Convention met in the Territorial House Chamber of the new capitol. The two-story room included a public balcony, a stained-glass lay light and a brilliant chandelier. The room is historical, for it was there that Wyoming reaffirmed the right of women to vote and included that right in the state constitution. The space also served as the chamber of the Wyoming Supreme Court and then housed the Legislative Service Office. Today, the historical Territorial House Chamber is once again restored as it was in 1889 and is a public meeting room. It is because of this room and the inclusion of women's suffrage in Wyoming's constitution that the Wyoming Capitol is designated as a national historic landmark.

On March 26, 1890, Wyoming's congressional delegate Joseph M. Carey introduced a bill calling for statehood. Because of its low population (estimated at around sixty-two thousand in 1890), there was some opposition in the U.S. Congress to admittance. Despite those protests, including an objection to female suffrage, Wyoming became the forty-fourth state admitted to the union on July 10, 1890.[2]

Wyoming remains one of the least populated states in the nation, with just over a half million folks calling it home. It is still possible to stroll into the state capitol and meet someone you know.

After many additions and upgrades, the latest and most major renovation project is slated to be completed as this book is published, insuring that the capitol's classical style and gold-leaf dome remain the focal point of Cheyenne. Author Starley Talbott recalls, as a rural school student, visiting the capitol on numerous occasions. Though no longer allowed, Talbott stated, "It was scary and exciting to ascend the steep and narrow curved stairs to the capitol dome and then peer out the tiny windows for a view of the city and far-off mountains." Author Linda Graves Fabian (formerly Linda Rollins) worked as a state employee for many years and recalled, "The Wyoming State Capitol building and grounds on a winter morning, with the trees covered in hoarfrost, was especially beautiful."

1

A Dream Rises from the High Plains

Before construction began on Wyoming's new capitol building, the territorial legislature met in rented rooms on Sixteenth and Seventeenth Streets in Cheyenne. The territorial governor, Francis E. Warren, appointed a five-member building commission consisting of chairman Erasmus Nagle, Charles Potter, Nathaniel Davis, Morton Post and Nicholas O'Brien. After the Capitol Building Commission selected an architect and a building contractor, ground was broken for a new house of state on September 9, 1886.[3]

David W. Gibbs of Toledo, Ohio, was selected as the design architect. Gibbs worked as a builder and a draftsman before establishing his architectural office in Toledo, where he designed the Masonic temple and the Soldiers and Sailors Memorial Building, among other structures.[4]

The construction contract was awarded to the firm of Adam Feick & Bro. of Sandusky, Ohio. The Feicks' company had completed several buildings in Ohio of similar style to what was desired for the Wyoming Capitol. Since the distance from Sandusky to Cheyenne was quite long, the Feicks subcontracted with Robert C. Greenlee of Denver to oversee the project. However, it was necessary for a member of the Feicks' company to reside in Cheyenne. George Feick initially traveled to Wyoming to inspect the project, but after returning to Ohio, it was determined that George's nephew and Adam Feick's son, John, would be sent to Cheyenne to manage the operation.

George wrote the following letter to John Feick:

David Gibbs, architect for the first phase and the first addition of the Wyoming Capitol, rides his buggy past the capitol around 1889. *Wyoming State Archives, Department of State Parks and Cultural Resources.*

November 26, 1886

Mr. Greenlee furnished good bond and think from present intimation all will go well as may be expected. I have made contract for cut stone. Have also completed contract for about 1½ million brick. The weather just now is bad but as soon as the weather is better things can move all right. I am getting prices on lumber by different home parties and will try Chicago on my way back. My present plans are as follows: I will engage a small house right near the Capitol building and expect you to move out here perhaps in February or March all depending some what on the weather. Will get all lumber and (nock down) frame here by the same time. You can easily take charge of all we have to do make the centers frame. Joist and put frames to gether. In fact one man can take all the wood work until the building is inclosed of course all the interior wood work will have to be prepared East and we can easily bring a few good men to put it up. This is a very lively town and you and your wife will like it very well. I think better than Oberlin or eaven Sandusky. As I have learned so far if a man wants to do the right thing the people will Stand by him. Think it would be well for you when in Sandusky to have some one file a application for you to the Masonic fraternity, as it will be of some use to you and will take you about two months to become a master mason. Will write you again from Chicago,

Yours as ever,
G. Feick

Several months passed before John Feick arrived in Cheyenne, and some of his work and activities will be explored through letters to his wife back in Ohio in Chapter 2. Meanwhile supplies were being gathered from many locations in preparation for the construction of the new capitol.

Some of Feick's letters were written to the company and concerned business, including the following:

Cheyenne, Wyoming
Feby 23, 1887
A. Feick and Bro.

Dear Sirs:

I must have sizes of Vault doors and would like to know if they are going in while wall is being built or if they can be put in afterward. You said I had a letter of the Carier Iron works giving the sizes, I have not, but have a coppy of the letter you wrote them asking for the size. You gave Greenlee the width but not the height, you had better wire us the height at once if you please. How are framers getting along? I have a good many creter made, Surads man has about 500 lbs of Bolts ¾ inch iron and about 6 ft. long which he does not need here, he says that we can have them for the freight, shall I take them? He maybe has not arrived home yet. The masons can only work 4 & 5 hours a day. I sometimes wait a lot hoping to hear from you soon.

I remain yours Respectfully,
John A. Feick

Cheyenne, Wyo
March 9 1887
A. Feick and Bro.
Sandusky Ohio

I received two of your letters this evening. I have no copy of the letter you wrote to Greenlee in regard to sizes of vault doors, so if you have the copy at home, if do you remember the width you gave Greenlee of vault doors. He made openings for vault doors 2 ft. 6 and they ought to be 2 ft. 10. I would like copy of letter you rote to G if can find it. We are getting along nicely and without quarrelling. I think the crews will get over being so precarious after they see the work going on faster, will write you again just as soon as I get a little quieter, it keeps me hustling to get along with the work at present.

Yours in respect,
John A. Feick
Mr. Naylor has no plans yet.

Apparently, John Feick stayed in rented rooms in several locations after arriving in Cheyenne, but at some point, he constructed a small building on the capitol grounds to serve as his living quarters. He called his temporary home "the castle" in some of the following letters:

Cheyenne Wyo
March 26 1887
A Feick and Bro.
Sandusky Ohio

I received a letter of inquiry from work and the Bill of Material that they sent in the two cars. The Commission telegraphed for Mr. Gibbs today and told him to come at his earliest date to make our estimate, would have telegraphed you but told maybe that this would reach you in time. Men could not work today it was very cold and stormy all day and is snowing tonight. We built 16 ft. more onto our shanty for framers. We have four steps and the platforms set on both fronts. Having no news I will close hoping to hear from you soon.

Yours as ever,
John A. Feick
It is devilish cold ice in our castle tonight.

In the following letter, John Feick discussed his conflicts with Erasmus Nagle, chairman of the Capitol Building Commission. Nagle was a prominent Cheyenne businessman and served as president of the Union Mercantile, a large grocery business. He also held positions of trust and authority in the community. Nagle was able to construct his own lavish residence by acquiring some material that had been meant for the capitol. The building contractor refused a large quantity of stone that was designated as inferior, so Nagle decided to use the stone to construct his own home at the corner of Seventeenth Street and House Avenue. He commissioned D.W. Gibbs, the master architect of the Wyoming Capitol, to build his mansion. The house was finished in 1888 and sported gas, electricity and six full bathrooms in addition to its many elegant refinements. Nagle died only two years after the mansion's completion. In 1910, the home was bought by U.S. senator Francis E. Warren. The building was later acquired by the YWCA and subsequently by other owners. Today, it remains a beautiful and historic Cheyenne building known as the Nagle Warren Mansion and serves as a bed-and-breakfast. The mansion was placed in the National Register of Historic Places on July 12, 1976.

Cheyenne Wyo
April 29 1887
A. Feick and Bro.
Sandusky Ohio

Father & George:

Mr. Nagle is bothering the devil out of me to make his houses. I told him time and again, we could not do it for him. He says we will have to do it because there is no one else that will suit him. He says if I had no time I should get a man from home for him and where ever I needed him at the Capitol I could have him, we will have to do something for he is after me all the time. It gives me no rest at all. I will see him about paying the man's fair back & forth, so that we can stand it, he will allow us a little commission on the man, send over Schafer if you can. Everything else is all right.

Yours as ever,
John A. Feick
Answer this as soon as you can.

It is not clear if a man was sent out from Ohio to help construct a house for Erasmus Nagle. John Feick was kept busy acquiring the proper materials for the capitol and discussing plans for the laying of the cornerstone, as expressed in the following letter:

Cheyenne Wyo
May 4 1887
Mr. George Feick
Sandusky Ohio

Dear Geo.

I received your letter this evening and was very glad to hear from you. I feel very lonesome since you are gone. I have kept very busy on account of measuring Rawlins Stone, that is never better than you think for, and takes considerable of my time. John G. has treated me very nice since you are gone. I have done the same to him, we will get busy on this estimate sometime tomorrow will send you copy of it in a day or two. Wish you could have stayed for the laying of the corner stone will have a big time. They have collected $1800.00 so far, they want to use some of our ⅞ inch lumber for tables to eat on, told them they could have the use of it for ten dollars a lineal ft. and if they cut any of it would cost them $12.00 a lineal ft. They want to make about one thousand lineal feet of tables 3 feet wide. They want the front fence moved about 200 ft. told them that I would do it for $50.00 that is for the fence only. They are going to have the Barber-Cue.

I want one of your pictures (Cabinet Size) to be put in the corner stone, wrote to father for one of his so be sure to have it here in time. Hoping to hear from you soon, I will close by sending my best wishes to all.

Yours as ever,
John A. Feick
P.S. Got a letter of Shilby in regard to his son this evening, the last I herd or saw of him, he was boarding at the Enter-Ocean, they moved the barrel today so I don't know where will board now.

As with most projects, it seems that John Feick and the team of contractors encountered the ups and downs of supervising a large undertaking. They had to deal with many subcontractors and businesses that provided goods and services for the building of the Wyoming Capitol.

Dozens of workers perch on the walls and in front of the building as they pose for the camera during the first addition to the capitol around 1889. *Wyoming State Archives, Department of State Parks and Cultural Resources.*

One of the major subcontractors was the Rawlins Dimension Sandstone Company, which provided most of the stone for the structure. Several items of correspondence between the Rawlins Company and various parties to the construction of the capitol have been saved in the Wyoming State Archives and read as follows:

Rawlins, Wyo., Feb. 23^d, 1887
Rob't C. Greenlee, Esq.
Denver, Colo.

Dear Sir:

Replying to your favor of the 20th, would state that on Saturday last we shipped you one car of stone. To oblige you, we put men at work in the quarry, and are loosing money on every car of stone we ship you.

I am today in receipt of a letter from Mr. Hamma, stating that the car has arrived, and the measurement was not satisfactory. This car of stone was measured at the quarry, and re-measured by our Mr. Galbraith after being loaded on the cars, and we are confident that the measurement was correct.

You well know that stone cannot at this time of the year be squared as well as it can be in the summer time; and as we are working at a great loss to comply with your wishes to keep your men going, we consider that we are asking no favor, but simply justice, when we ask you to instruct your men at Cheyenne to be liberal in their measurements.

We shall to-day or to-morrow ship two cars more, and would like you to instruct your Cheyenne foreman to measure the stone on the cars, and notify our agent (Mr. Hamma) of his measurement, so that we can arrange this matter of measurement satisfactorily.

We wish to deal liberally with our customers, but cannot help thinking that we are as capable of measuring stone here as parties in Cheyenne. I should be pleased to hear from you fully regarding this matter.

Yours truly,
J.C. Davis, Secy

⁓

Rawlins, Wyo., April 28th, 1887
Messrs A. Feick & Bro.,
Cheyenne, Wyo.

Gentlemen:

Please give us the number of pieces of stone that falls short of filling out 2x3, 2x1, and we will send others to take place of them.

The stone that is yellow will bleach out the same color as the other in a very short time. We have noticed this particular for the past two years.

All we ask is a fair deal. Where a stone fills the place it is ordered for in the building of course we expect the measurement, as you are aware, that in cutting so many small stones and handling them three times, it is impossible to get them there perfect; but we know that the quarry work is well done. We have a force of quarrymen from Canada just arrived.

Yours truly,
J.C. Davis, Secy

❧

Rawlins, Wyo., May 26th, 1887
Peter Hamma, Esq.,
Cheyenne, Wyo.

Dear Sir:

Your favor of the 25th inclosing check for $193.34 to hand, for which please accept thanks.

   Please tell Mr. Feick that we are about up on the orders sent us, and unless he furnishes us with the dimensions he requires we shall ship him large blocks of stone as per agreement with Mr. Feick who visited us.

Yours truly,
J. C. Davis, Secy

❧

Rawlins, Wyo., Aug. 3, 1887
Mess. A. Feick & Son,
Cheyenne, Wyo.

Dear Sirs:

Will you please have Mr. Greenleaf send us a list of the bills of the stone he will require for the completion of the Capital building. We have requested this from Mr. Greenleaf on three different occasions and he has failed to respond. I trust you will give this matter your prompt attention, as you know it is necessary for us to know what you require, some time ahead.

Yours respy,
J. D. Davis, Sec.

❧

Rawlins, Wyo., Sept. 7, 1887
Mess. A. Feick & Son,
Cheyenne, Wyo.

Dear Sirs:

*I am instructed to inform you that your representatives Mess. Greenlee &
Sons are not fulfilling their part of the contract, refusing to pay freight
weekly as per contract, neither have they remitted any money for last months
stone. I trust you will have them live up to their part of the contract, if they
expect us to.*

Yours respy,
J.C. Davis

⌒

Rawlins, Wyo., Nov. 23ʳᵈ, 1887
Messrs A. Feick & Bro.,
Cheyenne, Wyo.

Gentlemen:

*Replying to your Postal Card of the 21ˢᵗ, I beg to inform you that the
weather is so severe that we have been compelled to shut down at the quarry.*
*We have several cars of stone the sizes ordered by Mr. Greenly in the
yard ready for shipment.*
*As soon as the storm abates and we can get cars, the same shall be
shipped to you.*

Yours truly,
J.C. Davis, secy

⌒

Rawlins, Wyo., Dec. 22nd, 1887
Mssrs Greenlee & Son,
Cheyenne, Wyo.

Gentlemen:

I have waited several days before answering your letter of the 17th, thinking that the weather might be such that we might be able to do some more quarrying and send you more stone. I now have to inform you that it is impossible for us to quarry any more stone during such weather as we have, and consequently will not be able to send you any more until next season opens up, when we will be enabled to send it as far as you may need.

Yours truly,
J.D. Davis, secy

Other entrepreneurs in southeastern Wyoming and Cheyenne in particular submitted bids for work and supplies for the new capitol building. Here are some of the bids and invoices found in the Wyoming State Archives:

Cheyenne, Wyo., Jan 7th 1887
T.F. Dolan Dr.
Plumbing, Gas and Steam Fitting and Plumbers Supplies
Shop and Office Corner 17th and Hill Sts. (Invoice)

50 lb. Solder	*7.50*
Lead Tags	*5.00*
10 Wash Bowls	*15.00*
8 Marble Slabs	*80.00*
4 Urinal Stalls	*195.00*
4 Urinals	*25.00*
10 Basing Cocks	*15.00*
14 Santos Traps	*35.00*
4 Urinal Cocks	*6.00*
10 Days Plumber & Helper	*60.00*
Total Due	*$443.50*

Cheyenne, Wyo., Jan 14 1887
Bradley Brothers (Invoice) Contractors for All Kinds of Stone Work
Dec 16   3 Loads of Sand $2.70
Jan 2   5 Loads of Sand $3.75
Jan 4   2 Loads of Sand $1.50
Total Due $7.95

Cheyenne, Wyo, Jun 1 1887
Brush-Swan Electric Light Co. (Invoice)
1 Socket $1.25
1 Plug   .90
12ft of cable   .95
Misc.   .50 cents
Total Due $3.60

Cheyenne, Wyo., Sep 1 1887
Brush-Swan Electric Light Co. (Invoice)
To Light for the Month of Aug $1.25

Office of T.F. Dolan, Dr.
Plumbing, Steam Heating, Gas Fitting
Cheyenne, Wyo., March 7th 1887
Mr. A. Feick & Brothers

Gentlemen:

I the under signed do here by propose to furnish all material and labor for doing the Plumbing and Gasfitting and Electric light wires in the Capitol Building for Wyoming Territory according to the Plans and Specifications furnished by D.W. Gibbs & Co. Architects, Toledo Ohio.

For the sum of Thirty Seven Hundred and fifty Dollars ($3750.00)
Plumbing and Gasfitting only the sum of Thirty Hundred and fifty Dollars
($3050.00)
Electric light wire Seven Hundred Dollars ($700.00)

Resp Yours,
T.F. Dolan

∽

Cheyenne, Wyo., Oct 6 1887
Arp & Hammond Hardware Merchants
216 W. Seventeenth St. (Invoice)

Brought Forward	*$47.84*
2 Kegs Nails	*8.00*
Bench Screw	*.75*
2 Kegs Nails	*8.00*
1 Keg Nails	*3.75*
Oil Stove	*1.50*
Chest Lock	*1.25*
Oil Can	*.50*
Tin Bucket	*.40*
Total Due	*$71.99*

∽

Cheyenne, Wyo., Oct 7 1887
Cheyenne Transfer Co., J.S. Murray, Proprietor
Dealers in Hay, Coal, Wood and Ice
For Hauling Car Wood $9.00

∽

Cheyenne, Wyo., Dec 31 1887
Andrew Gilchrist, Corner of Eddy and 19th St., R.B. Horrie, Manager
Hardwood and Pine Lumber, Wagon Lumber, Shingles, Lath, Posts

Nov 15—14 pieces 2/6 & 20 pieces 2/6	*$12.43*
Nov 21—50 pieces 2/6	*23.20*
No. 23—760 lbs. of building paper	*19.07*
Dec 3—1000 ft. Pressed board	*28.00*
Dec 3—400 ft. 1x4 board	*10.00*
Total Due	*$92.70*

Even though work continued on the new capitol, it was not completed in time for the Tenth Territorial Legislature to meet in its proper chambers in 1888. However, the legislature met in the new building, and the house delegation convened in the Supreme Court Room of the new capitol. The council met in the rooms intended for the Wyoming Agricultural Department.

The Capitol Building Commission accepted the completed building from the Adam Feick & Bro. Company, and the commission submitted its final report on March 31, 1888. The territorial assembly had already passed a bill providing $215,000 for construction of additional public buildings including $125,000 for adding wings to the capitol.

Territorial governor Thomas Moonlight objected to the appropriation for more public buildings and for adding to the capitol. The disastrous winter of 1886–87 had brought hardship to the cattlemen, an industry that was an important economic pillar of Wyoming. Moonlight was concerned about the economy, and he vetoed the appropriations bill, providing the following reasons for the veto:

> *Now that business is depressed, with cattle companies breaking up and banks closing their doors, with poverty staring many a good man and woman in the face, and the list of uncollected taxes in the county for 1887 covering a whole page of the county paper, it is proposed to add to the already oppressive burdens of taxation, and for what purpose? The Capitol Building as it stands today is large enough for all the requirements of the territory for at least six years to come. The expenditure of a few thousand dollars to complete it within and fit it for occupancy would be wisely spent, and would receive the hearty endorsement of all the people, but I do not believe that the expenditure of $125,000 will meet the approbation, at this time, of one-third of the people.*

Moonlight's veto was overridden by members of both houses of the legislature, and he reluctantly appointed a second Capitol Building Commission. The commission selected David W. Gibbs as the architect.

It chose Cheyenne contractor Moses P. Keefe's bid of $117,504 for construction. The commission accepted the additional wings on April 4, 1890, and resolved, "We believe in this building are to be found greater room and comfort and more elegance and taste, than in any other structure of like cost in the United States." The completion of the second phase of the capitol was a cause for celebration, because on July 10, 1890, Wyoming became the forty-fourth state admitted to the Union.

Nearly twenty-five years later, the capitol was once again overcrowded, and plans were initiated to add more space to the building. Governor Joseph M. Carey stated in 1913,

> *The question of obtaining sufficient room to do the work that is required under the direction of the state officers has become a serious one. Every portion of the Capitol is now occupied. Some of the space used is not all adapted for the work for which it has been assigned. Some rooms have been secured outside of the Capitol, but this is not satisfactory, for the business done by the state should be concentrated.*[5]

Workers pose as the first wings of the capitol building addition near completion around 1889. *Wyoming State Archives, Department of State Parks and Cultural Resources.*

The legislature did not grant Carey's request, and it was not until 1915 that it agreed to provide funds for the construction of additional wings for the capitol. Governor John P. Kendrick reiterated Carey's plea for more space and added, "The congested condition of the Capitol Building, as suggested by Governor Carey at that time as a serious and urgent need, has today become an absolute and imperative necessity, and it is extremely important that prompt measures should be taken to relieve this condition." The legislature agreed and passed a bill providing for the addition.

The third Capitol Building Commission chose William Dubois of Cheyenne as the architect for the new wings. The contract for the construction was awarded to John W. Howard of Cheyenne for a bid of $140,790. Howard completed the wings on the east and west sides of the capitol on March 15, 1917. These wings serve both chambers of the Wyoming legislature, with the senate meeting in the west wing and the house of representatives meeting in the east wing.

Throughout the years, the capitol continued to undergo various changes within the interior of the building. One of the most interesting changes occurred on the second floor. Originally, this floor contained the Supreme Court Room, which measured thirty-six by forty feet and was twenty-six feet in height. The Territorial House of Representatives met there temporarily in 1869. It was in this room, in 1888, that the continuation of the women's suffrage movement, passed by the 1869 Territorial Assembly, was considered. After much argument, the representatives approved the women's suffrage movement, which was again discussed in the 1889 Constitutional Convention and agreed to by the delegates. This room later became the home of the Legislative Services Office. During the most recent renovations, this room has been restored to its original configuration and will serve as a public meeting space.

Beginning in 1974, the capitol was modernized with the addition of modern lighting, fire-rated surfaces, technical requirements and heating, plumbing and air-conditioning systems. Exterior work included restoration of masonry, rebuilding the dome and repainting of surfaces. The renovation was completed in 1980 at a cost of $7 million under the direction of Hitchcock & Hitchcock Architects of Laramie, Wyoming.

In 2014, after much deliberation, the Wyoming legislature agreed to a total renovation of the capitol. Construction began in 2017, resulting in the closure of the building for approximately two years. Space for government officials was rented in several locations throughout Cheyenne during the construction.

The interior of the Wyoming Capitol Building, showing three floors and the unique tile on the main floor. *Wyoming State Archives, Department of State Parks and Cultural Resources.*

2

THE LONELY SUPERVISOR

Twenty-five-year-old John Feick of Sandusky, Ohio, was dispatched to Wyoming Territory in 1887 to supervise the construction of the new capitol building in Cheyenne. Feick was the son of Adam Feick, partner in the firm of Adam Feick & Bro., who had won the contract for constructing the capitol.

John Feick first boarded with Cheyenne residents but later built himself a small abode on the capitol grounds that he called his "castle," from which he supervised the construction project. He wrote many letters to his young bride, Lizzie, back in Ohio that told of his exploits in Wyoming. Lizzie was unable to accompany her husband to Wyoming because she was taking care of her brothers and sisters while her widowed father was in Germany. Here is John's first letter to Lizzie from Wyoming Territory:

Feby 2, 1887

Dearest Wife!

I just arrived at Cheyenne right side up and handled with care. I tell you it was a long ride. I thought that I went around the world five times, can not tell you any thing about Cheyenne yet, just came in and is very dark, will write you a good long letter tomorrow which you will get Sunday morning if you go to the post office between 9 & 10.

John Adam Feick was the supervisor for the A. Feick and Bro. Company of Sandusky, Ohio, which built the first phase of the Wyoming Capitol around 1887. *John A. Feick III photo collection.*

It is snowing & blowing bad enough to scare a man to death the first night, would have written you from Chicago, or Omaha but train went right straight through.

Do not worry about me I will try & do the best I can I feel very lonesome & tired.

Yours,
John A. Feick

In John's next letter to Lizzie a few days later, he described his first impressions of Cheyenne:

February 5 1887

Dearest Wife:

I suppose you received the letter I wrote you when I arrived. I had quite a long trip, and feel very lonesome and homesick for you, to be fifteen hundred miles away from you and in a part of the country where you have to wear a belly-band to keep your cap on your head is a pretty bad thing.

There are very wealthy people living in this town but they all look to me like Cow-boys, Lizzie you can not imagine what kind of a country this is you can go just one hundred miles straight out in the country and not see a house or a living sole, but wolves, prarie Dogs, Deer, there are some very heigh mountains that you can see from Cheyenne that have snow on the top all the year around and the cars run to the top of them and that is 8000 feet heigher than Cheyenne. Cheyenne is just two and one half miles heigher in the air than Sandusky is, so you can imagine how the wind blows.

I will close for two night and write you another letter in the morning, hoping to hear from you soon.

Your true & faithful husband,
John A. Feick

John continued to write about his activities in Cheyenne in the following letters:

Feby 13, 1887

Dearest Wife,

I received your first letter and was glad to hear from you. I thought you would never write. I am well but terrible homesick, you asked where I was last Sunday, in the morning I had breakfast at 9 o'clock. Then Mr. Greenlee & I went out after Jack Rabbits. Came back at 2 o'clock and had Dinner. Then we took a walk around the town. Had supper at six. Then I went to church till half past nine, and then to Bed. I am stopping with Commissioners Nagle's Mother a very fine place and get my meals at the

Hotel. We have had very cold weather heare, 12 below zero, and the next day it would be so hot that I could not stand it with my under cloths on. We have some terrible winds heare will write you this evening again must go to Dinner.

Yours as ever,
John A Feick

❧

Feb 14, 1887

Dearest Wife:

I received another one of your letters and two papers this evening and was glad to hear from you. I see by the papers you have plenty of rain East… we never have rain here all the year around but we have some very queer weather in this country in the morning it is bitter cold from 10 to 2 o'clock in the afternoon the sun shines so hot that we are looking for shade and from 2 o'clock the wind will blow so hard that you would think the world was coming to an end. Sunday morning I was to church in the afternoon I went for a walk in the country had supper at six and then went to church again. We have some very nice churches in this city…

Yours as ever,
John A. Feick

❧

Feb. 17, 1887

Dearest Wife:

We had a fire here last night and the wind blew at the rate of 75 miles an hour and now are having a terrible snow storm but very little of the snow stays on account of the wind, I am getting a little over my being Homesick cause I get a letter or paper of you most every night. The mail comes in once a day and that is in the evening after supper. I was to see Katie Putman at the Opra House last night and was a very good show wish you could have been here to see it. I am getting aquainted with a good many very nice folks but have not been inside of a Saloon yet nor have I touched a drop of intoxicating liquor since I left home & don't intend to if I can holde it out which I think I can…

Your most affectionate Husband
J.F.

The young supervisor was indeed quite lonely in his new outpost in Wyoming, as indicated in the next few letters to Lizzie. He expressed how much he missed her and how hard it was to not be together for her birthday, and he assured her that his eye would not be turned by any other woman.

Feby 18, 1887

Dearest Wife:

I received your sixth letter of Feby 15 to night and was very glad to hear from you. The wind done considerable damage around here, a freight train of 48 cars was blown off the track about a mile from town all telegraph wires are down, yesterdays train was 19 hours late, the Denver passenger train that left here in the morning was blown of the track & rolled down a steep hill, 2 passingers were killed and a good many had their arms & legs broken. The roof was blown off of the Catholic Convent which is west to the Capitol it is a large four story building (Brick)…I am very sorry that I could not be home on your 20th Birthday, but still I thought of you all the time I wanted to buy you a small it was very pretty something new that I never saw before there were 4 nice gold leaves hooked together & looked very rich, but the price was to rich for my pocket Book $42.00 is what he asked and it was not longer than your little finger but it was a daisy, but never mind I love you just the same only take good care of your self…

Yours as ever
John A.

Feby 20, 1887

Dearest Wife:

The house that I wanted to get is rented to another man that was right close by the Capitol. Board is very high here I pay $10.00 ten dollars a month for my room and five & a half dollars a week for my meals, so that comes very high, Meals I get at the Restaurant and the room of Mr. Nagles mother the man was at Sandusky, I have a very nice room and a good bed so I can rest well at night. But sometimes I get so homesick for you that I think I must pick up and go home, but it can not be helped, you must not worry about me will try and take good care of myself you need not be afraid of me making a mash the women that are in this city are all homely, if I was to kiss one of them it would turn my stomach, have not seen a good looking girl yet…I will send you a newspaper from Cheyenne which you show to the boys and then you send it to your father which I think will interest him very much in telling old country people how they Brand Cattle in the Wild West send it as soon as you can that he will get it before he leaves there.

Yours as ever,
John A.F.

~⌐

Feby 22 1887

Dearest Wife:

The weather was very warm today and tonight it is 12 below zero. You can tell L. Kinzler that I am Boarding Mrs. O'Reiley's Hotel…You can tell Cap Brown if you see him that there is plenty of game in this country such as Deer, antelope, Jack Rabbits wolves etc and if he want to enjoy a good hunt, to come out here, give him my best regards. Cheyenne has about 15 thousand inhabitants. They were all enjoying Washingtons Birthday today. They have some finer stores here than there are in the East only that everything is very expensive and the only thing I buy here for the same price as I do East is postage Stamps…

John A.F.

Feby 23, 1887

Dearest Wife:

I was in the house all day last Sunday on account of bad weather, you asked if they have any saloons here, I can tell you the town is made up of Saloons but I have not stepped inside of one yet. I am very tired and homesick but feel very well otherwise...

Yours
John A.F.

John Feick's letters to his wife continued to talk about the weather, and one amusing story he told her was about his inability to wash his clothes or even the necessity of doing so.

March 1, 1887

Dearest Wife,

I received your letter of Saturday morn this evening and tomorrow night I will be here just one month but the one month seems to me like one year, we are have nice summer here for the last two days & hope it will stay so for some time. It seems very queer to see no snow in Cheyenne but a hundred miles distance you can see the tops of mountains covered with snow & does not seem more than two or three miles away, this is a queer country I tell you...You asked me if I had my washing done at the laundry, I have not had any cloth washed since I am here. The first day I struck town they told me any man that wore a white shirt would be shot, so I bought a blue sailor shirt or what ever you would call them in Ohio, I have not changed since nor have I had my Sunday cloth on since the day I struck town and the shirt will last 3 months longer with out changing, you will think that I am a Cow-Boy when you see me again...

Respectfully as ever,
John A.F.

~

March 9, 1887

Dearest Wife:

We have not had any rain since I am here but still have lots of wind. My cloths don't need washing yet and my socks have no bottom, but will get them washed and wear them as leggins I get shaved twice every week which costs 15¢ every time and 35¢ for a Hair Cut…You need not be afraid of me looking for another bed pardner as long as I am out here, They have plenty of bad houses out here but they do not bother me.

It is true what I told you about wearing white shirts. I wish you could be out here when the corner stone will be laid. The Free Masons are going to lay the stone and expect to have a grand time over it. I think George will be out when the time comes and if your father is at home then you can come with him…

Yours in haste
John A Feick

The lonely John Feick also seemed to have had some trouble being comfortable with the rooms he had been renting during his first few months in Cheyenne. At last he had devised a plan to build himself a small abode on the Capitol grounds where he would be more comfortable. He called his new quarters his "castle" or "palace."

March 12, 1887

Dearest Wife:

The mail is four hours late this evening so I can not get it until morning but will try and write you a little letter tonight. I am feeling considerable better today than I have been for some time. I will move to my new palace as soon as my blankets come I have it fixed up in grate shape inside I have four bunks two over each other, one for Chas. W., one for George when he comes, and one for myself and the other is a spare bed for company when we have any I got some coffee sacks filled them with straw and that makes a very good straw tick. On the West side in one corner I have my wardrobe for my choths & C next to that is my desk for my papers, Books & c.f. and in the west corner is my wash stand have a baisen, dipper, soap pail on it, under it a place for my shoe brush and blacking and other thrash and a room for a chamber but don't need any on the north side back of the door is the grand looking glass, towels, broom and C and on the South side is my trunck with shelves and c.f. over it, and in the center of the room I have a center table of my owne make. Monday the men are coming to put Electric light in my room, a lamp would have been good enough for me but the electric light is just as cheep and there is no danger with fire, the room is not very heigh just heigh enough so that I can stand up straight. I made it low on count of the wind, have two windows in the room with curtins on them so you can imagine what kind of a palice I have. If Chas. W. is not gone yet when you get this letter send two good towels and an old hair brush so that I can brush my hair once in a while. I will write you more about it & tell you how I like it when I live in it a while, my meals I shall get down town at Wilcoxes' the same as always. Having no news I will close hoping you are all well and that I may hear from you soon.

Yours as ever,
John A Feick

After moving to his new "palace" near the capitol building, John Feick seemed to be getting used to living and working in Cheyenne and let his wife know that things had improved.

March 15, 1887

Dearest Wife:

I begin to like this country better every day the grass is coming out green and the leaves are coming out on the trees, the air is so clear and pure that you can see one Hundred and fifty miles and see the snow on all the tops of Mountains. Mr. Nagle took me out for a ride last Sunday and I enjoyed it very much, he has a very fast team…They are blacks and are well mated and I tell you I rode just as fast as I ever want to ride in a buggy. You tell Chas Joe and Joe Lerman if they want to see nice horses and horses that are fast they should come out here. Mr. Nagle sold a horse to a Chicago man for six Thousand two hundred dollars last Saturday. He would not have sold her, but she was a terrible kicker and he could not drive her…This morning when I went to Breakfast I saw a Chinaman laying in the Street with his head cut off and it looked terrible.

You asked me in your last letter if I chewed I do and every body else in town even every little boy that can walk, there is something in the climate that makes people chew here so excuse me I never drink, they tell me the whisky a man gets here would make a man go home and rob his own trunk.

You don't see as many drunkards in Cheyenne as you do in Sandusky and the town is kept very orderly other wise I think you will like it when you come out, perhaps you can get your father to come out with you for a visit when he comes back. I know he would enjoy himself very much to go out on the ranches Sunday Nagle and I were on Arbuckles ranch that is 14 miles from town, he is the only man around here that raises sheep and has two hundred thousand sheep on his ranch (Arbuckle is the man that manufactures Coffee in the East) then we went to Posts Ranch and saw 18 Stallions that he Mr. Post got from France Europe last week, he told us he had over two thousand horses on his ranch and they are all well bred horses. Mr. Post has the largest horse ranch in the world, he says the 18 Stallions cost him Sixty two thousand dollars. I will close for this time hoping you are all well.

Yours as ever,
John A Feick

⁓

March 18, 1887

Dearest Wife:

…if you come I will not keep house but will board and sponge on the neighbors as a good many other people do. I shall stay until the building is finished if I keep well that is if you come out, if not I shall come home once to see you George will be at Cheyenne the First of April.

The carr came to Cheyenne this evening and will unload it tomorrow afternoon if everything goes all right. The apples you sent with Chas are very good. But I tell you the nicest thing we have in our shanty is the electric light we take in bed with us…

Yours as ever
John A. Feick

❧

March 19, 1887

Dearest Wife:

We got our carr unloaded this after noon and found the cake which pleased me very much and the sausage was emence you tell Charly that I am ever so much obliged for it. Mr. OBrine one of the Territory Commissioners says he never saw such sausage, he eat half a pice and wanted to take the other half to his wife he says he never eat any sausage that tasted better to him than that. The cake is good and did not dry up very much for which I am ever so much obliged…hoping you are all well…

Yours as ever
John A. Feick

❧

March 20, 1887

Dearest Wife:

I received your letter this evening and was very glad to hear you are all well. I will draw you a better picture of our room when I have a little more time. You can send towels that go on a roller and I will make a roller for them. Today I bought a stove and a large chair in a second handed store, 5.00 for the stove and 2.50 for the chair. Allmost every body in Cheyenne has been to my room to see it and think it is very comfortable little place…

Yours as ever
John A. Feick

❧

March 29, 1887

Dearest Wife:

I received your letter No 25 this eve but did not get any papers. If Katies sister could talk English she could get work here girls are very scarce in this country and get big pay for ordinary house work they get Twenty dollars (20) a month room and board and that is a big pay for a young girl.... The wind blew very hard today so that a person could not see their hand before their face...

Yours as ever
John A. Feick

As the date for the laying of the capitol cornerstone was fast approaching, John wrote again to ask Lizzie to come to Cheyenne for the big event and told her to insist to his business partners that she be allowed to travel to Cheyenne for the celebration.

Apr 2, 1887

Dearest Wife:

I received two of your letters this evening No 29 & 30 and was glad to hear from you. I got a letter of George saying that he was going to Denver Colorado and would not be in Cheyenne till Tuesday night, he is going there to see George Cooke & his wife. If George asks you again about comming out you tell him you insist on comming out or want me to come home, I know one thing that I shall not stay here alone all Summer if I can help it.... You must think I look terrible raggid the way you write I have lots of mending to do and keep my cloths in good trim.

Mrs. Nagle is going to take me to the Ranch tomorrow morning and we are going to stay all day to have a pick nick. Wish you could be here to go along. Having no more news I will close hoping you are all well which I am the same...

Yours as ever
John A Feick

Residents watch the laying of the cornerstone for the Wyoming Capitol on May 18, 1887. *Wyoming State Archives, Department of State Parks and Cultural Resources.*

Many of John Feick's letters mention having a meeting with Erasmus Nagle or that Emma Nagle has taken him exploring somewhere around the Cheyenne area. Mr. Nagle was the chairman of the Capitol Building Commission, along with the other members of the commission, Charles Potter, Nathaniel Davis, Morton Post and Nicholas O'Brien.

April 7, 1887

Dearest Wife:

I have not written to you for two or three days, have allways been busy during the day and at night time we were with the Capitol Commission or at Nagle's house so I did not get time to write, but am sorry for and will try and be a little more promt after this. George came Tuesday night and was very glad to see some one from Sandusky. Mr. Filbys son is out here too and seems to like it very well. The towels you sent me are very nice and so is the comb & brush for which I am ever so much obliged. George sleeps on the top bunk in our castle. I will close and write you more news tomorrow night.

Yours as ever
John A. Feick

⤳

April 11, 1887

Dearest Wife:

I suppose you think it queer, because I did not write to you this and last week as much as usual. George & I were off every night and was kept very busy. It is twelve oclock now, and just came home from Mr. Nagles. Sunday Mrs Nagle & I were out to the Herferd ranch all day and had a grand time & wished you were her very much....We are having very nice weather and am beginning to like this place very much. When you come I think you will have to move out here I think you will like it very much after you get aquainted.

Yours as ever
John A. Feick

⤳

April 25, 1887

Dearest Wife:

Chas & I were working at Nagles house for the last three days we had an awful snow storm here last Thursday, the snow was even with the top of our shanty and could not get out until we had shoveled our way out the snow was 15 & 20 feet in some places....Having no news I will close hoping you are well & that I may see you soon.

Yours as ever
John A. Feick

⤳

May 1, 1887

Dearest Wife:

I received your letter and papers and was very glad to hear from you. I was not feeling very well for the last two days. We had a terrible Snow storm last night and it is terrible cold today. We are going to have a grand time at the laying of the corner stone and wish you could come by the 18th of May, it will be something that you never see before the train is here and must get this mailed to go off…

Yours as ever
John A. Feick

⁓

May 2, 1887

Dearest Wife:

People here are going crazy over the cornerstone they have collected $1800.00 Dollars to lay it with, they are going to have a BarberCue, that is something that you or I never saw in the East, perhaps you don't know what a Barber Cue is, if you don't I'll not tell you what is until you come to see it. The People of Cheyenne have appointed me on two commitees on Committee of arrangements, and on the Committee of receptions, so you see I don't belong to you common people in Ohio any more, Inclosed find notice they sent me, was to the meeting tonight and had quite a time, Mrs. Nagle & Mrs Wilcox expect to see you by the 18th of May. If you come out here and stay till fall you can vote, all women have the right to vote when in the Territory 3 months. If the boys and the other children do not care, I wish you would bring Alfred with you, speak to Chas & Joe about it. I think it would do him considerable good, there are good & better Catholic schools here than there are in Ohio. Mr. Nagles little boy would like to have hime come very much he has a very nice little poney and buggy and is just about Alreds size, if he did not want to stay long he could go back by the first of Aug When George or one of the Commissioners went East.

Yours as ever,
John A. Feick

As it turned out, for unexplained reasons, Lizzie Feick was not able to travel to Cheyenne for the laying of the cornerstone at the new capitol. Her husband wrote to tell her about the exciting events that occurred in Cheyenne for the momentous occasion.

May 6, 1887

Dearest Wife:

I received your letters & papers tonight and was very glad to hear from you, but not that you was not coming out for the laying of the corner stone. We are estimating for May again so I do not get time to write long letters have to sit up half of the night to get through with my work. Having no news I will close hoping to hear from you again.

Yours as ever
John A. Feick

May 26, 1887

Dearest Wife:

I suppose by this time you know what kind of a time we had at the laying of the Corner Stone, people expect to have a larger time on Decoration day, I tell you this is a great country for excitement. People are more liberal & a nicer class of people than you find in the east. Train is here & I must close hoping to see you soon. Many kisses,

Yours as ever
John A Feick

John wrote to Lizzie on May 31, 1887, explaining the train schedules and how she should travel to Cheyenne. He wrote again the next day:

June 1, 1887

Dearest Wife:

I received your letter and papers and was very glad to hear from you…You rite that you all wondred what I was doing Sunday Mr. Nagle took me to the post in his buggy we had a nice time hearing the band play then we went to the fairgrounds & saw the Base Ball game.

Hoping you will get out all right & have a nice journey I will close hoping to see you soon. Many Kisses to you

Yours as ever,
John a Feick

Lizzie Feick traveled to Cheyenne to spend the next six months there before she returned to Ohio. There are no letters during this time period, but John Feick's letters resume early in 1888.

January 11, 1888

Dearest Lizzie:

I've received no letter of you yet and am patiently waiting for one to see how you got home and what all the folks thought when they saw you come in the door….We are having regular summer weather it is very warm. The town has considerable life in it since Lection day, than the Legislature met last Tuesday and the Street Cars run every five minutes, there are many strange people in town and everything is very lively about Chian…

Yours,
John A.

January 12, 1888

Dearest Lizzie:

Have received no letter of you yet but shurely aught to get one tonight or in the morning: We have had nice weather ever since you left but today it is blowing terrible hard the sand is blowing around so that a person can hardly see their hand before there face. I have no news at present only that I miss you a great deal & feel terrible lonesome and everybody else that sees me asks where you are. Will close this hoping to hear from you tonight.

Yours,
John A

January 17, 1888

Dearest Lizzie:

Just got home from the Capitol and now is half past eleven, Mr. & Mrs. Wilcox are drinking a Tom & Jerry on the head of the new mother—law. We work all last Sunday and every night [t]his & last week hense the delay of my writing. I think we will get home very soon so have a little patience and we will soon be together again....Sam Wilcox wants me to go in Business with him and will give me a good show. I am really on the fence & don't know what to do, but will want to go home once more and see all the folks & what father thinks about it. Of course I do not want to leave him if I am any help to him.

Your Dear John

Jany 22, 1888

Dearest Lizzie:

I received your letter this evening and was very glad to hear from you, we are all well at present & hope we will be until I get home. We have regular summer weather for the last five days and it seems so funney when you say that you go out sleighing in Sandusky.

The plasterers left on the new road tonight and wanted me to go with them the worst way, & said they would pay my fare If I would go with them, They will send us a dog (Pug) to Sandusky to my address so when it comes you will have to take good care of it until I get home. They hated to leave with out me but it will not be very long before I get home.

We worked hard all day at the Capitol we have second & third stories finished and have the dome very near finished then all there will be left is the basement & first story settling up, pack our trunk & tools, sweep out the building, have our trunks taken to the depot, buy our tickets, tell them all good bye, jump on the train, kiss my best girl, ride for two days and night on the train, then we are in Sandusky…

Yours,
John A

Jany 28, 1888

Dearest Lizzie:

I received a letter of you this evening and was very glad to hear from you, I did not write to you last night I was very tired and came home late tonight we did not work at the Building but I had to work at the office awhile tonight it is now ten oclock and being my Birthday is today I send Toney over for a Growler which we quietly are drinking on the head of the Birthday, we have got to work in morning so you cant expect much news of me tonight.

Yours
John A.

⁓

Feby 9, 1888

Dearest Lizzie:

Lizzie how would you like to move to Denver to live I think there's where I will spend my next summer I might just as well get out of Sandusky first as last and try my luck…

Yours
John A.

⁓

Feby 23, 1888

Dearest Lizzie

Dear Lizzie if everything goes right we will leave Chian about 4 weeks from next Saturday and be in Sandusky about the 28 of March and then wont we have a bulley time. I can hardly wate till time comes…

Yours
John A.

⁓

March 5, 1888

Dearest Lizzie:

I received all of your letters suppose you think I have forgotten you because I did not write for so long. The members of the Legeslature had an excursion to Denver and invited us along so George, Gerlach, Louey, and I went. We had a nice time. John Greenlee took me all around the town, and at night we went to the Tabor Opera house and saw Fantasnia it was a good show and we enjoyed it very much.

Yours
John A.

❧

March 13, 1888

Wife Lizzie

I think we can start for Sandusky a week from next Saturday if nothing happens so you can stop writing a week from tomorrow the 14/88 having no news I will close…

Yours
John A.

❧

March 14, 1888

Dearest Lizzie:

We will get done here just the time I have promised and all the men will go east just that time if nothing happens I will go to Salt Lake City if I possibly can so I will be home 2 or three days later, of course this may not be for certain but want to go very much if I can…

Yours
John A.

By the middle of March 1888, John was anxious to finish his work in Wyoming and travel back to Ohio to be with his bride. However, he did express regrets at leaving Cheyenne and even considered returning to Cheyenne to live and work.

March 17, 1888

My Dearest Lizzie:

I received your kind & welcome letter this evening and was very glad to hear from you. I am well & glad to hear you are the same, only that I am terrible homesick and anxious to see you all again. I suppose in a week from tonight by this time we will have all our tickets bought and on the train then I will be happy when two days are gone by so as to see Sandusky, but for some reason I hate to leave Cheyenne. I don't know why I am not very much stuck on the town but I hate to leave it.

Mr. Nagle wants me to stay here the worst way & says he will help in every way that he can Mrs. N. sends her best wishes to you…

Yours
John A.

March 20, 1888

My Dear Lizzie:

I received your letter & was glad to hear from you we are having lots of snow and bad weather, we will all be finished to go home Saturday, if I go to Salt Lake City you must not be angry with me for I would like to see it very much if I can work some skeame to get there without George knowing it. Mrs. Nagle sends her best wishes to you & wishes you were back again. I will telegraph you when I start for home…

Yours
John A[6]

John Feick's letter of March 20, 1888, was his last to Lizzie from Wyoming Territory. Though he had expressed a desire to move to the West, the couple remained in Sandusky, where John continued working with the family business and became the father of one son, John Charles Feick.

With the death of John's father in 1893, the business's name changed to George Feick & Company. In 1899, the National Sugar Manufacturing

Company hired the Feick Company to build its new mill, assorted outbuildings, houses, schools and almost the entire town in Sugar City, Colorado. John, Liz and John Charles visited the Colorado site.

In 1902, John Feick started his own business, John A. Feick Contractor & Builder. He loved the Lake Erie Islands and built the foundations for the Perry Peace Memorial Monument, a large hotel, businesses and a summer home for his family on South Bass Island. John Adam Feick died in 1930 at the age of sixty-eight. His son, John Charles, who had joined the business in 1913, took over the firm, which was later run by his son, Edward L. Feick. The business continues today under the names of Feick Contractors Inc. and Feick Design Group Inc.[7]

3

THE PEOPLE CELEBRATE

Much jubilation ensued at the laying of the cornerstone for the construction of the capitol in Cheyenne on May 18, 1887. Dignitaries and ordinary citizens gathered to celebrate the momentous occasion.

The *Cheyenne Daily Sun* reported that the laying of the capitol cornerstone was "the occasion of the greatest military and civic demonstration ever witnessed in the history of the city."

Preparations for the celebration had taken weeks. A team of workers constructed a temporary cookhouse, tables were set up west of the capitol, and a fifty-foot-long barbecue pit was dug nearby. Cheyenne banks and businesses closed their doors at noon on May 18, and soon after, a grand parade wound its way through the streets of the city. The parade consisted of troops from Fort D.A. Russell, bicyclists, bands, firemen, territorial and city officials and many different groups of citizens.

As the crowd gathered, the Masons took their positions on a temporary platform built at the cornerstone to the left of the capitol entrance. The cornerstone, a fine piece of Rawlins sandstone, hung suspended by a derrick. Underneath was a copper box that held items such as the laws of Wyoming, an impression of the great seal of the territory, various territorial newspapers, timetables of the Union Pacific Railroad and several photographs.

After the copper box was placed under the cornerstone and the stone was in place, the crowd was addressed by several dignitaries. Judge Joseph M. Carey (who later became Senator Carey) gave a momentous speech on the early history of Wyoming and remarked that the capitol should be "devoted to those of wisdom, good government and righteous law, which hereafter shall be enacted within it." Governor Thomas Moonlight added his words to the occasion, and the *Sun* stated that he "made a very happy address which was frequently interrupted by applause."

Following the dedication ceremony, the crowd thronged to the barbecue, where it dined on pork, mutton, roast beef, bread, cornerstone pickles and lemonade prepared under the direction of T.W. Ashford. The *Sun* reported that "the fare was unusually good and tasted all the better from the fact of keen appetites and being eaten out of doors. Several hours were thus occupied, relays of people rapidly following each other." In the evening, the Irish Benevolent Society hosted a grand ball with dancing "kept up until an early hour."

The capitol was not completely finished until March 1888, but the celebration in 1887 provided citizens with a sense of pride in the new building overlooking the city park. The capitol building was a modern structure with plumbing, electricity, gas, water and heating and ventilating systems. The interior woodwork was cherry from Sandusky, Ohio. The limestone used in the foundation and steps came from Fort Collins, Colorado, while the sandstone in the superstructure was from a quarry in Rawlins, Wyoming.

A large crowd was on hand for the celebration of the laying of the cornerstone and to partake of the barbecue in 1887. *Wyoming State Archives, Department of State Parks and Cultural Resources.*

The Capitol Building Commission submitted its final report on March 21, 1888, but plans had already been made to add two wings, which were completed by April 4, 1890. The commission stated that "we believe in this building are to be found greater room and comfort and more elegance and taste, than in any other structure of like cost in the United States."

Even further celebrations of enormous joy followed when Wyoming attained statehood on July 10, 1890. News of the Wyoming statehood bill's passage in the U.S. House of Representatives on March 26, 1890, brought a great outburst of cheering throughout Wyoming.

Church bells, train whistles, fire bells, cowbells and trumpets sounded in Cheyenne. That evening, a huge bonfire blazed at the corner of Seventeenth Street and Ferguson Avenue (later Carey Avenue), after which a crowd gathered at the opera house to hear speeches. Three months later, on June 27, the U.S. Senate approved the statehood bill. Again there was an impromptu parade in Cheyenne with clanging bells, shrieking whistles and yelling. President Benjamin Harrison signed the statehood bill on July 10, 1890, setting off yet another celebration the following day. There were the usual bells and whistles accompanied by firecrackers in Cheyenne; a forty-four-gun salute was fired in Laramie; cannons boomed in Rock Springs; Douglas celebrated loudly; a wild celebration ensued in Rawlins; and Buffalo reporters said that "the great north is delighted."

The official celebration of statehood occurred in Cheyenne on July 23, 1890. The formal observance was attended by nearly five thousand people and included a two-mile parade featuring troops and bands along with many carriages and floats. On one large float rode forty-two young women representing the older states. It was followed closely by a small carriage in which rode three little girls representing the goddess of liberty, the state of Idaho (admitted July 3) and the state of Wyoming. The parade led to the capitol, in front of which a large throng had gathered for the principal program of the day.[8]

Theresa A. Jenkins offered the first speech, a review of the struggle for women's suffrage. The *Cheyenne Leader* stated the next day that her address was the most forceful and eloquent of the day, although it conceded that at one point she was carried away by a "fairest and rarest flight of oratory."

Some excerpts from Jenkins's speech include:

> *In behalf of the ladies present and in the name of many who are not with us today, I am requested to make this expression of our appreciation of the great benefit conferred upon us at your hands, and confirmed by the*

The view from the Union Pacific train depot in Cheyenne looking north toward the capitol on Capitol Avenue. *J.E. Stimson Collection, Wyoming State Archives, Department of State Parks and Cultural Resources.*

Congress of these United States. Happy are our hearts today, and our lips but sound a faint echo of the gratitude within our bosoms. While we rejoice with you that our young commonwealth has been permitted to place upon this beautiful banner her bright prophetic star, how much more reason have we for enthusiastic demonstration.

The republican spirit of 1890, with a generosity unrivaled in all the annals of political economy, has admitted into the national jurisprudence, the voice of woman. We have been placed upon the very summit of freedom and the broad plain of universal equality. Think ye that our tongues are silent or that we have no need to sing our anthems of praise? History chronicles no such an event on all its pages, and the bells of the past ring out no such victory.

We have never been compelled to petition or protest; we have ever been treated with a patient hearing and our practical suggestions have been most courteously received and in the future we but desire a continuance of these favors. We ask of our law makers just laws for the enlargement and perpetuity of our educational facilities; we ask of our legislators wise and magnanimous measures for the erection and maintainance [sic] of our benevolent institution; we ask of you laws for the better protection of the moral as well as physical natures of our boys and girls, even though the maverick be neglected, and, taxpayers and burden bearers that we are, may we not expect the proper enforcement of these laws as well as the framing of them. We have, it is true, many lessons to learn and possibly many mistakes to make, but shall we not choose for our instructors those have had our best interests at heart, who seeing the need may plan for the result. We, no doubt, will be advised by many factions, some declaring we are behind in our social and moral reforms, others that we outspeed [sic] public sentiment, but the experiment is ours, and with us it will succeed or fail....

Bartholdi's statue of liberty enlightening the world is fashioned in the form of a woman and placed upon a pedestal carved from the everlasting granite of the New England hills, but the women of Wyoming have been placed upon a firmer foundation and hold a more brilliant torch....

These words of thankfulness would be incomplete were we to neglect to utter the sentiments of our hearts in enumerating among our noble friends the names of the framers of our constitution...and in this galaxy of stars which every woman wears to day a diadem of gems shines out, the fairest and rarest of them all, F.E. Warren and J.M. Carey, and ye who applaud say never again a prophet has honor save in his own country....

And may that beautiful bow of color which spanned our eastern boundary at the golden sunset hour of July 10, 1890, be but a faint promise of the prosperity, the stability, the harmony of our magnificent domain, guided (not governed) by the hand of man clasped in the hand of woman.[9]

Fifty years later, Jenkins's daughter recalled for the *Wyoming State Tribune* that her mother had been heard by everyone in the audience, which extended to a point four blocks away, because she had practiced on the open prairie, with her husband riding off in a buggy to greater and greater distances and shouting back at intervals, "Louder."

The ceremony progressed with the presentation by Esther Hobart Morris of a forty-four-star silk flag to Governor Francis E. Warren. Several speeches followed, with the program ending with the oration of the day by Clarence D. Clark, an Evanston attorney, in the absence of Senator Joseph M. Carey, who could not be present. Clark had been one of the leaders of the Constitutional Convention and later served as a U.S. senator. The evening ended with fireworks nearby and a grand ball in the capitol.[10]

The *Cheyenne Daily Sun*'s July 24, 1890 Illustrated Edition reported on the event as follows:

"Wyoming's Day"
It was a grand day for Wyoming. This will be the verdict of all who witnessed the imposing ceremonies of yesterday. The Sun despairs of doing anything like justice to the celebration, and this morning's issue must be regarded only as a hasty and imperfect tribute to the occasion. The fact is that the preparations and consummation has surpassed the expectations of those who were most concerned about the success of the celebration. Many hands and many minds were at work and all have done their part so handsomely that we have no space for special mention, and must be content with giving a brief description of what transpired.

The visitors to Cheyenne have one and all been inspired with the zeal and patriotism shown in yesterday's demonstration, and their compliments are frequent and emphatic. On the other hand our citizens deeply appreciate the generous manner in which their neighbors came to the front on this occasion and most cheerfully acknowledge that their attendance contributed greatly to the enthusiasm of the day.

The ladies, God bless them, were out in all their beauty and glory, contributing by their bright smiles and gay colors, very largely to the life and eclat of the demonstration. They seemed to realize that the celebration was equally theirs and it was generally remarked that the portion of the exercises assigned to them was carried out in a manner that did honor to the occasion. Conspicuously so was the able and eloquent address of Mrs. J.F. Jenkins which was delivered in the open air, upon the steps of the Capitol to an assembly of over six thousand people, all of whom could distinctly hear every word that she uttered. Her remarks were sensible and to the point, and applause was frequently elicited by her noble sentiments and well rounded periods.

Hon. M.C. Brown delivered a neat and appropriate speech in connection with the presentation of a handsomely bound copy of the constitution to the ladies of Wyoming through their representative Mr. M.E. Post, who made an eloquent response.

Mrs. Esther Morris presented on behalf of the ladies of Wyoming, the beautiful silk flag, with considerate remarks and the response by Governor Warren, on the part of the territory, was fully up to the occasion, eliciting hearty applause both from the ladies and gentlemen.

Later on came the oration of the day, an earnest, eloquent tribute to Wyoming and her future, by the gifted and brilliant orator of western

Wyoming, Hon. D.D. Clark. Commencing in a modest, quiet manner, it soon became evident by the noble sentiments that he expressed and his masterly delivery, that the committee of arrangements had made no mistake in their choice of speakers.

The poem by Mrs. I.S. Bartlett is a gem and we publish it entire. We also wish it were possible to reproduce the grand chorus, which under the management of Prof. Pasmore was vouchsafed a delighted audience.

All who were so fortunate as to hear those soul stirring strains will treasure the great musical event in their memories.

We have only hurriedly touched upon the more important exercises of the day, but elsewhere will be found as a full report as we are able to present. As stated in the outset of this article, we only hope to give the readers of The Sun who were not present an approximate idea of the grand celebration of Wyoming's advent to statehood.

One hundred years later, in July 1990, folks gathered at the Wyoming Capitol to celebrate the state's centennial and to re-enact some of the events of the original statehood celebration. Governor Mike Sullivan officially instituted Wyoming's centennial celebration on July 10 by re-enacting the speech given by Governor Francis E. Warren in 1890. Others participating in the ceremony included Ruth Strike, granddaughter of Theresa Jenkins, representing Theresa Jenkins (prominent suffrage leader and speaker in 1890); Georjean Taylor, great-great-granddaughter of Esther Hobart Morris, representing Esther Hobart Morris (first woman justice of the peace); Jack Meldrum, nephew of John Meldrum, representing Judge M.C. Brown (head of the Constitutional Convention); Mary Mead, member of the Wyoming Centennial Commission, representing Mrs. I.S. Bartlett (prominent suffrage leader and poet of the day); John Brewster, great-grandson of Joseph M. Carey, former governor and U.S. senator, representing the Honorable C.D. Clark (prominent attorney from Evanston and leader at the Constitutional Convention); state senator Win Hickey, chairperson of the Statehood Day Celebration, representing Amalia Post (prominent suffrage leader); Father Carl Beavers, representing Father F.J. Nugent, who gave the benediction at the 1890 event; and Reverend James L. Green, representing Reverend J.Y. Cowhick, who gave the invocation in 1890. Music was provided by Amy and Annie Smith, Mary Jo Morandin, the Wyoming State Band and Capital Chorale.

At the conclusion of the re-enactment ceremony, a buffalo barbecue was served reminiscent of the meal served on Statehood Day in 1890.

The capitol around 1903, after the first addition was completed with a boardwalk leading to the front entrance. *Wyoming State Archives, Department of State Parks and Cultural Resources.*

Entertainment and tours continued throughout the day with a grand finale staged at Frontier Park. Loren "Teense" Willford served as master of ceremonies, and music was provided by Chris LeDoux and the Western Underground Band. The Wyoming Air National Guard provided a flyover with the posting of the colors and singing of the national anthem. Following speeches and introductions, the Sixty-Seventh Army Band performed, and the celebration closed with fireworks and a laser-light extravaganza.

Two weeks later, during Cheyenne Frontier Days, the Laramie County Centennial Committee replicated the original statehood festivities with the Centennial Parade. John Brewster, parade chairman, and Marietta Dinneen were the leaders of the effort to provide refurbished wagons to replicate the original parade vehicles. Bill Dubois—from the Wyoming Centennial Commission and grandson of William Dubois, architect of the third capitol addition—was the grand marshal of the Centennial Parade. Others in the parade included state officials, congressional delegates, Centennial Commission members, floats, bands and citizens on foot and horseback.[11]

4

GOVERNORS, LEGISLATORS AND OTHER LEADERS

The new capitol soon became overcrowded, making it necessary to add more space. New wings were added in 1890 and in 1917. Cheyenne architect William Dubois was selected for the 1917 addition, and the building contract was awarded to John W. Howard of Cheyenne at a cost of $140,790.

The addition of these wings provided space for both chambers of the Wyoming legislature, with the thirty-member senate meeting in the west wing and the sixty-member house of representatives in the east.

A ca. 1916 view of the Wyoming Capitol. *Wyoming State Archives, Department of State Parks and Cultural Resources.*

The main entrance to the capitol is on the south side of the Renaissance Revival building. The entrance leads into the central rotunda, which features a floor of checkerboard marble and the base of the dome directly overhead with its stained-glass imagery.

On the right of the rotunda is the original governor's office. There have been nine territorial governors and thirty-two state governors, though not all were housed within the capitol. The governor's office has been relocated to the east wing following the 2019 renovation of the capitol.

Following are the profiles of some of the people who have occupied this esteemed office in the Wyoming Capitol.

GOVERNORS

John A. Campbell

John A. Campbell served as the first territorial governor of Wyoming from 1869 to 1875. *Wyoming State Archives, Department of State Parks and Cultural Resources.*

The first territorial governor, John A. Campbell, who was appointed by President Ulysses S. Grant, arrived by train in the pouring rain at Cheyenne on May 7, 1869. Cheyenne was described as a drab, treeless place that had been established because of its location on the transcontinental railroad route. Campbell was aware of the importance of the railroad in the new territory, and two days later, he rode a train west to Utah to make sure Wyoming was represented at the Golden Spike ceremony marking the completion of the route.

Governor Campbell was born in Salem, Ohio, on October 8, 1835. He joined the Union army in 1861 and later served during the post–Civil War Reconstruction in Virginia. He served as Wyoming territorial governor from 1869 to 1875. The first job facing the new governor was similar to the work Campbell had done in Virginia of drawing legislative districts and setting up elections. The new territory was divided into five large counties running from the southern border of the territory to the north. Campbell, a Republican, had his challenges dealing with the real power in

Wyoming, the Union Pacific Railroad. He stood up to the railroad leaders when they tried to select candidates for the U.S. Congress as well as the legislature when it tried to repeal votes for women. Campbell left Wyoming in 1875 after accepting a job in the U.S. State Department.[12]

Thomas Moonlight

One of Wyoming's most controversial territorial governors was Thomas Moonlight, who was appointed by President Grover Cleveland on January 5, 1887, and served until April 9, 1889. Moonlight had served in the army and been stationed at Fort Laramie in Wyoming Territory in 1865. His stint as governor was immediately plunged into controversy. It had become the practice in Wyoming for cattle barons to illegally fence off public lands for the grazing of their cattle. Small landowners had protested this process, called "land grabbing" for the purpose of establishing a monopoly among the large cattle operators. President Cleveland had expressed his belief that public lands were not to be fenced by cattlemen and that the public domain should be available for actual settlers. Governor Moonlight was interested in the cause of the pioneer farmer and pledged to break the political power of the cattle ranchers.

The new territorial governor planned to change the economic and political character of the territory and encouraged immigration and economic diversification. The large cattle ranchers had built their wealth by exploiting the public domain, and they were not happy with the stance of Governor Moonlight. Thus began the governor's crusade against the cattlemen, which lasted his entire administration. During the winter of 1886–87, heavy snow and cold lasted for long periods, and cattle losses were disastrous. Governor Moonlight was not interested in assisting the cattlemen to recover from their losses, further deepening the divide between the governor and the ranchers. Wyoming's cattle barons felt the governor had forsaken them in their period of greatest need, many became his political opponents, and a few became his personal enemies.

Governor Moonlight also established poor relationships with the board of trustees at the University of Wyoming, and much controversy ensued over appointments at the university. He also had difficulty working with members of the legislature. Among other bills, the legislature passed one for the erection and maintenance of public buildings that Moonlight found to be too extravagant and he felt would retard settlement due to a large tax burden for residents. He also tangled with legislators about the formation and administration of new counties.

Wyoming's citizens desired to request admission into the Union, but Governor Moonlight was disappointed that his economic diversification and immigration policies had not been fulfilled. He opposed statehood, stating that there was not sufficient population and that "Wyoming is not ready for statehood."

Having antagonized the stock growers, the friends of the university, the legislators and the advocates of statehood, Moonlight's governorship was in trouble. These groups joined the Republican territorial organization in a crusade to remove the governor and

Thomas Moonlight served as the territorial governor of Wyoming from 1887 to 1889. *Wyoming State Archives, Department of State Parks and Cultural Resources.*

replace him with former governor Francis E. Warren. The election of Benjamin Harrison as president in 1888 brought about the appointment of Warren on March 29, 1889, and the turbulent administration of Thomas Moonlight came to a close.[13]

Francis E. Warren

Francis E. Warren served as both territorial governor and as the first elected governor of Wyoming. He was appointed territorial governor by President Chester A. Arthur, serving from 1885 to 1886, and again by President Benjamin Harrison from 1889 to 1890. He became Wyoming's first elected governor when Wyoming became a state in 1890.

Warren was born in Hinsdale, Massachusetts, on June 20, 1844, and lived with his family on a farm. He served in the Civil War in 1863 and then returned to farm for a short time, but he became fascinated with the lore of the West. He worked in railroad construction before boarding a Union Pacific train bound for Wyoming Territory, arriving in Cheyenne in May 1868. He worked in a hardware store and ending up buying the business in 1877. In the fall of 1883, he formed the Warren Livestock Company, a large cattle and sheep operation that eventually grew to 150,000 acres. He also owned the Cheyenne & Northern Railroad and the Brush-Swan

Electric Company, which provided the first electric power to Cheyenne.[14]

The young entrepreneur was elected to a two-year term in the territorial legislature at the age of twenty-nine. He was appointed as the territorial governor in 1885 and again in 1889. Warren was an advocate for statehood and wrote to the interior secretary that "the people of Wyoming want statehood. Men who have braved all the perils of pioneer life, have laid broad and deep the foundation of future homes, town and cities, and have treasured up the means that is to uphold the commonwealth, are not unmindful of the advantages of state government."

Warren was inaugurated as the state's first governor on April 9, 1890, but resigned on November 24 to accept a seat in the U.S. Senate, where he served as a prominent

Francis E. Warren, the first elected governor of the state of Wyoming in 1890, also served two terms as the territorial governor from 1885 to 1886 and 1889 to 1890. *Wyoming State Archives, Department of State Parks and Cultural Resources.*

Republican for nearly four decades. Among other committee assignments, Warren served as chairman of the Senate Military Affairs Committee and was instrumental in promoting Cheyenne's Fort D.A. Russell as a full regimental post. On January 1, 1930, Fort D.A. Russell was renamed in honor of Warren, and it was designated as Francis E. Warren Air Force Base in 1949. He was also known as one of Wyoming's "Grand Old Men."[15]

John Osborne

Wyoming's third governor, John Osborne, provided a rather colorful chapter in the state's history. Osborne was born in Westport, New York, on June 19, 1858. He graduated from the University of Vermont in 1880 with a degree in medicine and hired on as a surgeon with the Union Pacific Railroad.

Osborne moved to Rawlins, Wyoming, where he became successful as a doctor and in the pharmaceutical and livestock industries. In the early 1880s, a gang of outlaws roamed around southeastern Wyoming stealing horses and robbing trains, banks and merchants. One of these outlaws, known as "Big Nose George" Parrott, was tried on several crimes and executed by hanging in Rawlins in April 1881. Dr. Osborne claimed the corpse for medical study and subsequently made a death mask and a pair of shoes from the outlaw's skin.

A few years later, Dr. Osborne ran for governor, and he was elected on November 8, 1892, to fill the vacancy in the office created when the first elected governor of Wyoming, Francis E. Warren, resigned to become a U.S. senator. Osborne appeared to have won the election for governor as a Democrat, though ballots from Fremont and Converse Counties were delayed in being counted. The acting governor, Amos Barber, did not officially confirm Osborne's victory after several weeks of controversy. Osborne, not willing to wait any longer, had himself sworn in by a notary public on December 2 and moved into the governor's

John E. Osborne became the third governor of the state of Wyoming in 1893. *Wyoming State Archives, Department of State Parks and Cultural Resources.*

office. The Democratic *Cheyenne Daily Leader* applauded Osborne's actions, while the Republican *Cheyenne Daily Sun* accused him of usurpation and reported that he broke into the office through a window during the early morning hours, claiming he "displayed the agility of a trained monkey." There was much mudslinging in the newspapers before Osborne eventually became the official governor. Osborne continued his defiance of normal social behavior by wearing the pair of shoes made from the outlaw George Parrott's skin to his 1893 inauguration. To this day, the shoes are displayed at the Carbon County Museum in Rawlins, Wyoming.[16]

Joseph M. Carey

Another prominent Democrat, Joseph M. Carey, served Wyoming in several capacities. Born on January 19, 1845, to a Pennsylvania farm family, Carey earned a law degree in 1867. He was an active politician and worked on the presidential campaign of Ulysses S. Grant.

Carey arrived in the territory in 1869 when President Grant rewarded Carey with an appointment as U.S. district attorney for Wyoming. Two years later, he became the U.S. associate justice to the Supreme Court of Wyoming, a position he held until 1876. Carey also served on the U.S. Centennial Commission and as a commissioner at the World's Fair in Philadelphia. Carey was elected mayor of Cheyenne, was active with the Wyoming Stock

Growers Association and the Stock Grower's National Bank of Cheyenne, and served as a delegate to Congress for Wyoming Territory.

During his term in Congress, Carey authored the bill to admit Wyoming to statehood. Though he could not be present for the official celebration of Wyoming's statehood on July 23, 1890, he arrived in Cheyenne a few days later to an enthusiastic crowd, as reported by the *Cheyenne Daily Sun* on Sunday, July 27, 1890:

The news that Judge Carey, Wyoming's last delegate to congress, was to arrive home yesterday noon, created a spontaneous feeling of enthusiasm throughout the city and by one universal and common impulse, citizens of every class and degree turned out to meet him and give him a right royal welcome. Before the train arrived the immense platform of the Union Pacific station was a surging mass. Mechanics, artisans, business men and professional men left their avocation and rushed to the depot. The Union Pacific band marched down the street playing their most inspiriting music, and entertained the waiting multitude. The train arrived on time and as Judge Carey stepped from the cars a grand rush was made by the enthusiastic crowd, all eager to grasp the hand of the man whose untiring labors, earnest faith and devotion had done so much to place the new star of statehood upon our country's flag. While the hearty handshaking was going on the band played welcoming airs and round upon round of cheers rent the air. Silken badges were worn by hundreds, some inscribed "Welcome Joseph M. Carey, July 26, 1890," and others "State of Wyoming—44." Everyone seemed thrilled with enthusiastic delight. As soon as the numerous personal greetings were over Judge Carey was conducted to a carriage, the band was called and placed in front and the crowd insisted on falling into line and escorting the gentleman to his residence. The line of march was then taken up, the band struck up "Marching Through Georgia" and the grand army moved up Capitol avenue, along Sixteenth street to Ferguson and up Ferguson to Judge Carey's residence. All along the line of march there was cheering, singing and jolly remarks interchanged with bystanders. Everybody was happy.

On arriving at Judge Carey's residence the line divided in two ranks, through which the judge was escorted to the house. On his reaching the portico, three times three rousing cheers filled the air, the band struck up anew and the judge with evident surprise stood gazing upon the audience around him. It was a demonstration of which any man might feel proud and grateful. As soon as quiet could be restored the judge with difficulty mastering his emotions addressed the audience.

Here is a portion of Judge Carey's speech to the crowd, according to the *Cheyenne Daily Sun*:

Ladies and Gentlemen, I cannot find words to express my feelings at the warm, hearty and generous welcome which you have given me today, and as I once more step into my own home I can truly say I am glad to meet you. I am glad to be home again among my friends and neighbors, and I am profoundly grateful that I can greet you in the new state of Wyoming. When I left you a few short months ago I left behind me a territory, a dependency, a province. I now return and plant my feet upon the solid foundations of a state—a state invested with all the powers, prerogatives and privileges of the oldest states of the Union, the equal and the peer of any. I greet you as the free men and women of an independent, sovereign state. I am happy that the auspicious day has come when I can rejoice with you, and we can rejoice together over what has been accomplished—the realization of our most daring hopes and proudest anticipations.

Statehood has been achieved only by our strong, earnest and untiring efforts against powerful opposing forces. The young bark, Wyoming, was launched upon the troubled seas. It encountered storms, it was rocked amid fierce waves, it ran upon sand bars and rocks of congressional objections, but in defiance of winds and waves the good ship sailed safely into harbor, unfurled its flag and displayed its glorious banner with a new star upon it….

I thank my friends most cordially for your very kind and hearty welcome. I am with you today to take you by the hand, as a citizen, a neighbor and as one of the people, to help uphold the destinies of our state and to labor for its welfare with you, until it shall be one of the best, proudest and greatest states of our common country.

Carey was elected as the first U.S. senator from Wyoming in 1890 and served until 1895. Senator Carey sponsored the Carey Arid Lands Act, providing for cession of federal lands to states on the condition that they would be irrigated. Carey and his partners, William C. Irvine, Horace G. Plunkett, John W. Hoyt, Morton E. Post, Francis E. Warren and Andrew Gilchrist, were instrumental in establishing the Wheatland Development Company and an irrigation project to bring water from the Laramie River to the Wheatland Flats in the late 1800s. The Wheatland Development Company established water rights for thousands of acres of farmland near Wheatland, Wyoming. The company did not own the land, only the water

Left: Joseph M. Carey was a delegate to Congress for Wyoming Territory and the first U.S. senator from Wyoming from 1890 to 1895. He was the eighth governor of Wyoming from 1911 to 1915. *Wyoming State Archives, Department of State Parks and Cultural Resources.*

Below: Joseph M Carey *(center)* in front of the capitol with dogs, horses and men in uniform around 1910. *Wyoming State Archives, Department of State Parks and Cultural Resources.*

rights. Homesteaders had to acquire the land through the Carey Desert Entry Act, which allowed anyone over twenty-one years of age to claim 640 acres of land. The Carey Act required application of water to the land to obtain a patent. When proof was made, the settler received a patent for the land directly from the State of Wyoming, and when full payment was made for the water right, a deed was issued.[17]

After his term in the Senate, Carey was elected as the eighth governor of Wyoming, serving from 1911 to 1915. Joseph M. Carey was said to have been one of the most outstanding governors in all of Wyoming history. He understood Wyoming problems, knew what he wanted to do about them and asked for bipartisan support in developing the resources of the state and improving the state's institutions. Carey, who died on February 5, 1924, was often referred to as one of the "Grand Old Men" of the state of Wyoming, along with Francis E. Warren and John B. Kendrick.[18]

John B. Kendrick

An adventurous twenty-two-year-old Texan, John B. Kendrick embarked on a historic journey in 1879. Kendrick was born on September 6, 1857, and was orphaned as a child. When he was a young man, he rode horseback on the trails bringing herds of cattle from Texas to Wyoming. He worked on many Wyoming ranches and eventually established his own ranch and home in Sheridan, Wyoming.

Kendrick became president of the Wyoming Stock Growers Association in 1909. By 1910, he had become one of the most prosperous men in Wyoming's northern Sheridan County. A lifelong Democrat, Kendrick first became interested in politics from local participation in the entities of the Wyoming Stock Growers Association. He became a state senator from Sheridan County in 1911.[19]

News reports from 1914 claimed that when Kendrick campaigned for governor, he appealed to all segments of the population because he de-emphasized party affiliation and talked to the voters not as a candidate but as an ordinary citizen. He served as governor from 1915 to 1917. As a Democrat, Governor Kendrick established state workmen's compensation and a public utilities commission and worked to extend women's rights.[20]

Following his term as governor, Kendrick served three terms as a U.S. senator, representing Wyoming in the Senate until his death on November 3, 1933. His legacy to Wyoming included helping to uncover the illegal leasing

Left: Governor John Kendrick at his northern Wyoming ranch around 1895. He was Wyoming's governor from 1915 to 1917 and served three terms as a U.S. senator from Wyoming. *Wyoming State Archives, Department of State Parks and Cultural Resources.*

Below: The inauguration of Governor John Kendrick as he speaks from the front steps of the capitol in 1915. *Wyoming State Archives, Department of State Parks and Cultural Resources.*

of Wyoming's oil reserves in the Teapot Dome Scandal of the 1920s. He worked to bring water to Wyoming agricultural interests by advocating for the Alcova, Seminoe and Pathfinder dam projects. He also championed the protection of Wyoming's Yellowstone National Park. It was said that Kendrick became a successful Democratic politician in a Republican state because of his humorous charm, thick skin, broad intelligence and cheerful willingness to collaborate with political opponents.[21]

Nellie Tayloe Ross

Wyoming claimed national recognition when Nellie Tayloe Ross became the first woman to take the oath of office and serve as governor of a state on January 5, 1925. She was born in St. Joseph, Missouri, educated in public and private schools and moved to Cheyenne after her marriage to William B. Ross. Upon the death of her husband, who had been elected governor in 1922, Nellie Ross was nominated as the Democratic candidate for the unexpired term of the governorship. Though she faced competition from the Republican candidate, Eugene Sullivan, she was elected. Former governor and U.S. senator John Kendrick spoke on her behalf, saying "how fitting it was that the Equality State be the first to elect a woman governor."[22]

Nellie Tayloe Ross, governor of Wyoming from 1925 to 1927. She was the first woman governor in Wyoming and the nation. *Wyoming State Archives, Department of State Parks and Cultural Resources.*

The headline in the January 5, 1925 *Wyoming State Tribune* stated, "Nellie Tayloe Ross Becomes Wyoming's Governor at Noon Monday with Simple Ceremony." According to the *Tribune*, Nellie Ross was dressed all in black for the ceremony and delivered a brief statement including these words: "My election calls forth in this solemn hour my deepest gratitude, and challenges me to rise to the opportunities for service thus made possible, and to dedicate to the task before me every faculty of mind and body with which I may be endowed."

The first invitation to step onto the national scene came from Nellie's friend Eula Kendrick, wife of Senator John Kendrick. The request from

Eula arrived less than two weeks after Nellie's inauguration and urged her to attend the upcoming presidential inauguration of Calvin Coolidge. Nellie would be Eula's guest in Washington, D.C., and she was also invited to speak at a dinner for the Woman's National Democratic Club.[23]

Nellie accepted the invitation to attend the inauguration and rode in the inaugural parade. The *Washington Post* described the sensation Nellie created during the parade, where she was dressed in mourning garb of black velour, in these words: "The honors in the procession went without doubt to Governor Nellie Ross of Wyoming....She received applause all along the line....Guests in all the special seats rose to pay homage to the first woman governor to ride in an inaugural parade."[24]

As governor, Nellie Tayloe Ross was a champion of women's rights and stressed the need for tax relief for farmers. She proposed legislation to require counties, school boards and the state council to prepare budgets and publish them before levying taxes.

Governor Ross attended the National Governors Conference in 1925 and offered to host the 1926 Governors Conference in Cheyenne. Nellie was successful in securing the conference, which was held in conjunction with Cheyenne's annual Frontier Days celebration. Twenty-five governors traveled to Wyoming to participate in the meeting, again earning Wyoming public attention and praise.[25]

Nellie Tayloe Ross was defeated for re-election in 1926 by the Republican candidate, Frank Emerson. Following her defeat, she embarked on a career of writing and speechmaking on the national Chautauqua circuit. Presidential candidate Al Smith appointed her vice chair of the Democratic National Committee (DNC) in 1928. She was drafted to make one of his nominating speeches at the national convention that same year, and she even received thirty-one votes herself for the position of vice president. She directed the DNC Women's Division for the next four years, and she helped to direct the campaign for the women's vote both in 1928 and 1932.[26]

In 1927, Governor Nellie Ross wrote several articles for *Good Housekeeping* magazine entitled "The Governor Lady." Reminiscing about her term as Wyoming's governor, Ross wrote,

> *There are no leisure moments in the life of a woman governor, but neither are there any dull ones....Usually I arrived at the Capitol between nine and ten in the morning, and more often than not I was still there at six in the evening....The normal duties of the office included meetings of the important boards which administer the public lands of the state, direct the*

The National Governors Conference party in front of the Wyoming Capitol, July 1926, during the tenure of Governor Nellie Tayloe Ross. *Wyoming State Archives, Department of State Parks and Cultural Resources.*

various state institutions, pass on applications for farm loans, and supervise the fiscal affairs of the state.

Nellie went on to say that she received invitations to make addresses in cities far and near. She stated, "The people naturally want to see and know their Governor, and I regarded it my obligation, and a privilege as well, to acquaint myself by personal contact with their needs and desires in every part of the state. Accordingly, whenever possible, I accepted invitations to the dedications, celebrations, and conventions held within our own boundaries."

Governor Ross expressed her admiration for the people of Wyoming and her love for the state with these words:

In every little town and settlement, in the lonely homestead as well as in the large ranch, in the tang of the sagebrush even, and in the brilliance of the Indian paintbrush, Wyoming's state flower, flaming on the hills, I found delight…often at a turn in the road there would suddenly burst upon my view long stretches of beautiful and fertile valleys. Checkered with fields of varied crops, they looked like cross patch quilts, and I was as proud of their productivity as if I had cultivated every patch with my own hand. My chief pleasure, however, was in the interesting companionships that always awaited me at the end of the journey.

Concerning her defeat for re-election, Nellie Ross stated, "Though I failed of re-election by a small margin, I have no regrets, nor would I now, if I had the campaign to wage over again, modify my policy, except in one respect. Instead of ignoring some of the baseless and base charges that either insidiously or openly were disseminated throughout the state, I would myself refute them from the public platform."[27]

Following the 1932 presidential election, Nellie Ross was appointed by President Roosevelt as director of the U.S. Mint in 1933, where she served for

Governor Nellie Tayloe Ross *(second from left)* with three former Wyoming governors *(left to right)*, U.S. senator F.E. Warren, former governor Robert Carey and Senator John Kendrick, in front of the Wyoming Capitol around 1925. *Wyoming State Archives, Department of State Parks and Cultural Resources.*

Nellie Tayloe Ross *(right)* consulted with her assistant, Edness Kimball Wilkins, during Nellie's twenty-year service as the director of the U.S. Mint. *Wyoming State Archives, Department of State Parks and Cultural Resources.*

twenty years. Nellie selected Edness Kimball Wilkins from Casper, Wyoming, as her personal secretary at the mint. Wilkins served in that position from 1933 to 1947, and she and Nellie forged a good working relationship and became close friends.[28]

Nellie Tayloe Ross remained in Washington, D.C., following her retirement from the mint and stated, "I am grateful for all that the wonderful people of Wyoming have done for me." Nellie Ross died in 1977 at the age of 101 and was buried next to her husband, William, at Lakeview Cemetery in Cheyenne.[29]

Leslie Miller

In 1892, Leslie Miller moved from Kansas to Laramie, Wyoming, where he attended public school and the University of Wyoming. He held positions with railroad companies, the State of Wyoming Land Office, and the Wyoming Committee of the Fuel Administration Division. He served in the

U.S. Marine Corps during World War I and then became the president of Chief Oil Company.

Miller worked in business and politics within the Democratic Party and served in the Wyoming legislature for three sessions. He was elected governor in 1932 to serve the last two years of Governor Frank Emerson's unexpired term (Emerson died from influenza at the age of forty-eight). Miller was reelected in 1934 and served until 1939.

The Wyoming Democratic Party favored a sharp reduction in costs of state and local governments and urged the elimination of all nonessential state activities. During his first term as governor, Miller took a salary cut and declined to move into the governor's mansion. Major pieces of legislation enacted during his tenure were the adoption of a 2-percent sales tax on retail purchases and an act providing for state wholesaling of liquor through the Wyoming Liquor Commission.

Governor Miller was passionate about raising dahlias, and he planted and maintained a flower garden on the capitol grounds. Governor Miller's daughter, Katherine Mabee, recalled that before becoming governor, her father ran a service station in Cheyenne where he attracted customers by offering those who bought five gallons of gas a dahlia bulb and six gladiola bulbs. Mabee said her father continued to garden hundreds of dahlias and

Governor Leslie Miller presides over ceremonies for National Cheese Week at the Wyoming Capitol around 1935. *Wyoming State Archives, Department of State Parks and Cultural Resources.*

Governor Leslie Miller was an avid gardener. He is shown with the dahlias he cultivated on the grounds of the Wyoming Capitol around 1935. *Wyoming State Archives, Department of State Parks and Cultural Resources.*

gladiolas at his home on Pershing Street, where he would often pick the flowers each day to take them to the hospital or a business.[30]

As governor, Miller was described as being frank, straightforward, outspoken, courageous and stubborn. In August 1937, the *Wyoming State Tribune* said of him, "His judgment is not infallible, but if it's his considered judgment he stands by it. He does not maintain a closed mind, may be convinced by reason, facts and circumstances, but he is about as difficult to drive as a Brahma bull."

Miller ran for a third term in 1938 but was defeated. After his terms as governor, he worked for the War Production Board and served another term in the Wyoming Senate.[31]

Lester Hunt

Wyoming became the home of Lester Hunt following his service in the U.S. Army Dental Reserve Corps in 1919. Hunt established a dental practice in Lander, Wyoming, and became involved in local politics. He was elected as a Democrat to the Wyoming House of Representatives in 1932. He served as Wyoming's secretary of state in 1934 and 1938, and he served as governor from 1943 to 1949.

Important legislation that was enacted during Governor Hunt's term included a retirement system for teachers and the authorization of a bipartisan interim committee to study state fiscal practices. Hunt vowed to eliminate all nonessential spending and succeeded in cutting large amounts from appropriations bills.

Along with many Wyoming citizens, Governor Hunt and other officials warned of the dangers of federal bureaucracy and resented the interference of the federal government. One example was their opposition to the establishment of Jackson Hole National Monument near Grand Teton National Park in northwestern Wyoming. After years of opposition, the monument was abolished, but most of the land involved was included in Grand Teton National Park.

As governor, some of Hunt's other accomplishments included helping people acquire jobs and receive rural mail delivery. He was noted for helping people individually and received many letters of thanks from those he had assisted. Governor Hunt expressed a love for Wyoming with these words spoken at the fiftieth anniversary of statehood in 1940: "Times may change, but the fundamental character of Wyoming will never change. There will

A view of the capitol and the surrounding area, with buildings to the south and the airport to the north, around 1950. *Wyoming State Archives, Department of State Parks and Cultural Resources.*

always be the brightness of its sunshine, the pureness of its air, the music of its winds, the grandeur of its mountains, the inspiration of its forests, and the peace and security of its wide open spaces."

Hunt was elected to the U.S. Senate in 1948. He had described himself as a "liberal and a progressive but not a radical." He gave strong support in the Senate to public housing, an enlarged health program and federal aid to education.

However, political problems plagued the Congress during the era of Senator Joseph McCarthy, who conducted an anticommunist campaign against many citizens. Senator Hunt was described by his peers as a "gentle giant of a guy" who nevertheless stood up to McCarthy in the Senate and opposed him at several congressional hearings. As the 1954 election neared, Hunt was blackmailed and asked not to run again by McCarthy and others. The threat was based on the arrest and prosecution of Hunt's son for soliciting homosexual prostitution in Washington, D.C. After much deliberation, it was reported that Hunt withdrew from the election. A few days later, June 19, 1954, he committed suicide in his Senate office in Washington, D.C.

The reasons for Hunt's suicide remain uncertain. Many Wyoming citizens had written letters of support asking Hunt to remain in the Senate race. Among them, historian T.A. Larson wrote, "I believe that you have served Wyoming most conscientiously and effectively. You deserve a hearty 'Well done' from all of our citizens."[32]

Milward L. Simpson

Following the years of success of Democratic governors, there followed a lengthy period of leadership from Republicans. Milward L. Simpson became a prominent Republican leader and served as governor of Wyoming from January 3, 1955, to January 5, 1959. Simpson was born in Jackson, Wyoming, in 1897. Raised on the Wind River Indian Reservation, he worked as a coal miner, day laborer, cowboy and a semiprofessional baseball player. He served in World War I, earned a degree from the University of Wyoming, graduated from Harvard Law School and was admitted to the Wyoming Bar in 1926.

Princess Bluewater with Governor Milward and Mildred Simpson. Princess Bluewater was a revered leader of the Oglala Sioux Nation. Born in 1880, she traveled with Buffalo Bill's Wild West Show and was a frequent visitor in Cheyenne. *Wyoming State Archives, Department of State Parks and Cultural Resources.*

Simpson was elected governor in 1954 and helped to establish the division of mental health, initiated an increase in school funding and higher state salaries, approved a civil rights bill and secured federal authorization to build the first uranium mills in Wyoming. He was known as a take-charge governor and was a great promoter of Wyoming. The *Wyoming State Tribune* said of Simpson, "His enthusiasm and zeal for all things Wyoming knows no bounds."

However, he incurred the wrath of residents in his hometown of Jackson. Wyoming had a 1901 statute prohibiting gambling, but it had not been enforced in some communities. Simpson intervened in 1955 by obtaining the resignation of the Teton County sheriff, suspended several liquor licenses, and ended gambling in the popular tourist town of Jackson. Business leaders in town lamented that "Jackson's tourist industry was doomed."

Simpson was rated as one of the best governors in Wyoming history and described as being personable, energetic, forthright and courageous. Despite his popularity, he was defeated in the 1958 election by Democrat Joseph Hickey. Simpson later went on to serve in the U.S. Senate.[33]

Clifford P. Hansen

Another Wyoming native, born in Teton County on October 16, 1912, Clifford P. Hansen became Wyoming's Republican governor in 1963 and served until 1967. Hansen was prominent in promoting Wyoming agriculture, and members of his family were pioneers who had homesteaded and settled in the Jackson Hole area. Hansen graduated from the University

Governor Clifford Hansen on a quarter horse at the Wyoming Hereford Ranch east of Cheyenne. He served as governor from 1963 to 1967. *Wyoming State Archives, Department of State Parks and Cultural Resources.*

of Wyoming in 1934 and later became a trustee of the university. He was elected to the Wyoming Senate in 1937 and governor in 1963. Hansen's grandson Matt Mead became Wyoming's thirty-second governor.

During Hansen's term as governor, Wyoming became the twentieth state to adopt a right-to-work law. There was much controversy during legislative debates, and the galleries were crowded with citizens on both sides of the measure. Governor Hansen requested the National Guard to stand by in the capitol basement during the final debate and vote.

Following his term as governor, Clifford Hansen became a U.S. senator in 1967 and held that position until 1978.[34]

Stanley K. Hathaway

Stanley K. Hathaway, born in 1924, was a graduate of Huntley High School and the University of Nebraska. He served in the U.S. Army Air Force in World War II. After completing military service, he established a law practice in Torrington, Wyoming.

Hathaway served two terms as Wyoming's Republican governor from 1967 to 1975. During his eight years in office, Hathaway was concerned with economic growth and government reorganization. He urged larger appropriations for the Natural Resources Board and the Travel Commission, which he deemed the state's two principal promotional agencies in attracting business and tourism to Wyoming. Under Hathaway's leadership, the legislature maintained that the federal government had become too powerful and that it would be stopped only by making the state economy and government strong.

Governor Stanley Hathaway greets two unidentified children at the governor's office in the Wyoming Capitol around 1970. *Wyoming State Archives, Department of State Parks and Cultural Resources.*

The Republican governor promised that state government would dedicate itself to creating a congenial environment for business growth. However, he also recommended the enactment of legislation designed to protect the quality of Wyoming's environment. Hathaway believed that water laws should be modified to recognize recreation as a beneficial use of water. He also implemented the Department of Economic Planning and Development with four divisions dealing with water, industrial, mineral and planning concerns.

During Hathaway's second term as governor, the Legislative Service Office, the Department of Administration and Fiscal Control and the Department of Environmental Quality were created. The legislature also approved the construction of a new governor's mansion to replace the old one, built in 1904.

During Hathaway's tenure as governor, he was dedicated to growth and reorganization. By the end of his eight years, he left the state house as one of Wyoming's most popular leaders. He was appointed secretary of the interior by President Gerald Ford in June 1975 but resigned soon after due to ill health. He later resumed his law practice in Wyoming.[35]

Edward Herschler

A Wyoming native born in 1918, Edward Herschler served as the state's only three-term governor. Following his military service with the U.S. Marine Corps during World War II, Herschler graduated from the University of Wyoming. He then became the Kemmerer town attorney and Lincoln County prosecutor. He served as president of the Wyoming Bar Association and as executive secretary of the State Democratic Central Committee. Herschler was elected governor in 1975, and he held the office until 1987.

Governor Herschler worked to strengthen the Department of Environmental Quality and advocated for effective taxation of energy industries, stronger human services programs, state development of water resources, repeal of the right-to-work law and increased support for education at all levels. During his tenure, one of

Governor Edward Herschler served as Wyoming's only three term governor from 1975 to 1987. *Wyoming State Archives, Department of State Parks and Cultural Resources.*

his top priorities was to obtain funding for capital facilities construction. These facilities included a new state penitentiary at Rawlins, several remodeling projects at the University of Wyoming in Laramie, and several remodeling projects in the capital city of Cheyenne. He also oversaw the reorganization of the Health and Social Services Department, giving needy senior citizens larger tax rebates and increasing retirement benefits for state employees.

As a Democrat, Governor Herschler struggled to maintain his priorities, because the state legislature was controlled by Republicans throughout his three terms. But he worked behind the scenes and relied on friendships he had established in both parties dating from his ten years in the legislature.[36]

Governor Herschler is fondly remembered as one of the most likeable and unpretentious governors in Wyoming. Those who worked for him often loved to tell "Gov. Ed" stories. Dick Skinner, Herschler's former administrative assistant, recalled one of those anecdotes:

> We were in Douglas for the Wyoming state Fair in 1978 and the governor wanted to attend the Charlie Pride Night Show. I was not interested and since we had only one car, I agreed to drop the governor off at the fairgrounds and pick him up when the concert was over. So I went downtown and promptly forgot about it. About 10 p.m., I thought I better get back to the fairgrounds, where I discovered that the night show was over, the lights were turned off, and no one was to be found. I called the hotel and Gov. Ed answered the phone. I asked how he had gotten back to the hotel. He told me he hitched a ride with a couple of guys in a pickup truck, sitting on a bale of hay in the back of the truck, riding back to the hotel. I might have been fired had I been working for any other governor.[37]

Mike Sullivan

A smoky-colored and well-worn cowboy hat was the hallmark feature of Wyoming's twenty-ninth governor. Born in the small town of Douglas, Wyoming, the engineer turned lawyer never planned to run for public office, but he became one of the state's most beloved politicians.

Sullivan served two terms as governor, from 1987 to 1995. His tenure coincided with a bust economy, forcing him to navigate falling oil and gas prices, growing environmental awareness and increased unemployment. He held a reputation for bipartisanship in working through the issues facing the state.

Governor Sullivan presided over the festivities honoring the centennial celebration for the state of Wyoming in 1990. During the statehood

Right: Governor Mike Sullivan, wearing his well-worn and recognizable grey cowboy hat, was the twenty-ninth governor of Wyoming and served as U.S. ambassador to Ireland. *Wyoming State Archives, Department of State Parks and Cultural Resources.*

Below: At the signing of Conrad Schwiering prints benefitting the Wyoming Historical Foundation are *(seated)* Governor Mike Sullivan and *(standing from left to right)* Governor Clifford Hansen, Linda Rollins Fabian, Governor Edward Herschler, Dona Bachman, David Kathka and Governor Stanley Hathaway. *Wyoming State Archives, Department of State Parks and Cultural Resources.*

re-enactment ceremony on July 10, Governor Sullivan re-enacted the speech given by Wyoming's first elected governor, Francis E. Warren, and participated in various activities throughout the celebration.

In 1995, Governor Sullivan addressed the University of Wyoming graduating class in part with these words: "Wyoming is known for its independent minded people, its rugged beauty and its incessant wind. We value our independence and freedom of choice, but we also know when to depend on someone else. Wyoming is where cooperation isn't just a matter of being neighborly, it can also mean survival."[38]

President Bill Clinton appointed Sullivan as U.S. ambassador to Ireland, a position he held from 1999 to 2001. His Irish heritage helped him feel comfortable in that position, and sporting his cowboy hat all over Ireland made him immediately recognizable and extremely popular.

The former Wyoming governor was lauded by the National Western Stock Show in Denver, Colorado, as the 2016 Citizen of the West. The *Denver Post* lauded Sullivan for this honor, saying, "There is a slight air of self-deprecation to the man, not always common in a politician. It speaks to his reputation as someone who could reach across the aisle and find middle ground with opponents."[39]

Cheyenne historian and author Larry Brown honored the former governor by imagining what Mike Sullivan's well-worn hat might have had to say about its former owner with these words: "Well, I learned right quick that there are no surprises with Mike. He's honest, true and a friend, indeed, to those in need. And he don't cut slack for those who won't pull their weight. Best of all, he takes you as you are, even, as in my case, you're somewhat worse for wear." Former Governor Mike Sullivan's Stetson hat is part of the Wyoming State Museum's general history collection.[40]

Matt Mead

Wyoming's thirty-second governor, Matt Mead, took office in 2011. He was raised on the family ranch in Teton County. He earned a law degree from the University of Wyoming, practiced law and served as U.S. attorney from 2001 to 2007, prior to running for governor. Contributions to the state of Wyoming run deep in Governor Mead's family. His grandfather Clifford Hansen served as governor and as a U.S. senator. His mother, Mary Hansen Mead, was active in many state-level organizations, including service as president of the Wyoming Centennial Commission. She competed unsuccessfully for governor against Mike Sullivan.

During Governor Mead's two terms in office, he worked to establish and improve public access to technology, innovation and expansion of business opportunities. He maintained an online journal where he reflected on various aspects of being in office and his daily activities. He was known to be accessible to his constituents by maintaining an open-door policy and speaking at numerous events throughout the state. One of his speeches was to welcome all those attending the Great American Solar Eclipse, which passed through Wyoming in August 2017.

Governor Mead served as cochairperson of the Capitol Building Rehabilitation and Restoration Oversite Committee. The committee was created during the 2014 state legislative budget session to oversee all components of the Capitol Square Renovation Project.

Governor Mead reflected on his eight years in office by stating in his online journal, "It captures the respect and love I have for Wyoming and the people of Wyoming, and I am honored to have served as governor of this great state."[41]

Legislators

Wyoming's Constitutional Convention met in the newly minted capitol in September 1889. All of the fifty-five delegates to the convention were men. Women had been granted the right to vote and to hold office in Wyoming, but none had been elected to the legislature when it met in 1889.

Melville C. Brown, a lawyer from Laramie, Wyoming, became president of the convention. He stated that the delegation represented all the business interests of the state—bankers, stock growers, merchants, farmers, gold miners, coal miners, railroaders and lawyers.[42]

A great deal of the constitution of Wyoming was borrowed from those of other states, mostly from North Dakota, Montana and Idaho. On the twenty-fifth day of the convention, the constitution was adopted and signed by the delegates. The Laramie County delegation hosted the members of the convention at a banquet at the Cheyenne Club that night. At a special election on November 5, 1889, Wyoming voters approved the constitution.[43]

Many of the legislative delegates served their term and went home to continue their business interests. Some served more terms in the legislature, were elected to other offices or served in the U.S. Congress.

The Wyoming legislature is currently a ninety-member citizen legislature, meaning the people elected serve part-time and this is typically not their primary occupation. Wyoming remains one of the few states that have a true part-time citizen legislature. While the part-time nature of the institution allows members to stay in close contact with their constituents, it also means that they do not enjoy the same accommodations provided to full-time legislators in larger states, such as personal staff. The legislature meets in

Legislators and clerks in the Senate Chamber of the Wyoming Capitol, ca 1961. *Wyoming State Archives, Department of State Parks and Cultural Resources.*

General Session in odd-numbered years, beginning on the second Tuesday of January and lasting for forty days. In even-numbered years, the legislature convenes in Budget Session, beginning on the second Monday of February and typically lasting twenty days. Special sessions may be called at any time by the governor or the legislature.

While many outstanding citizens have served in the legislature or as other officials, here are the stories of some of the more notable persons elected to serve Wyoming:

WYOMING'S FIRST WOMAN LEGISLATOR

Mary Godat Bellamy

Mary Godat Bellamy was the first woman to be elected to the Wyoming legislature. She served two terms, the first in 1910 for two years and the second in 1918 for two years.

Mary Godat had moved to Laramie, Wyoming, in 1873. She attended Laramie High School, became a teacher and taught in Nevada and Wyoming. She married Charles Bellamy of Boston, Massachusetts, in 1886. He was a civil engineer who received the first license to practice engineering in the state of Wyoming and served as the first water commissioner.

As early as 1888, Mary Bellamy ran for county superintendent of schools in territorial Albany County, and she was elected to that office in 1902. When she was chosen to serve in the legislature, she supported issues affecting the welfare of women and children.

Mary Godat Bellamy was the first woman legislator in Wyoming, serving two terms in 1910 and 1918. *Wyoming State Archives, Department of State Parks and Cultural Resources.*

She sponsored changes to Wyoming's probate laws that allowed women to serve as administrators and executors. She supported bills that created industrial education programs and raised the mill levy for the University of Wyoming. Legislation to implement changes in the treatment of both female and juvenile prisoners incarcerated in Wyoming penal institutions was also among her interests.

An active member of the Council of Women Voters and a friend of Carrie Chapman Catt, prominent suffragist and founder of the League of Women Voters, Mary Bellamy was Wyoming's envoy to the national rally for women's suffrage in 1917. The University of Wyoming granted Mary a doctorate of law degree in 1952. She continued a life of service in Laramie and Wyoming until her death on January 28, 1955, at the age of ninety-three. She had received an honor from her husband, Charles, when he named a lovely lake in the Snowy Range Lake Marie during his work as a state engineer.[44]

WYOMING'S FIRST BLACK LEGISLATOR

William Jefferson Hardin

William Jefferson Hardin was the only African American to serve in the Wyoming territorial legislature, first in 1879 and again in 1882. *Wyoming State Archives, Department of State Parks and Cultural Resources.*

William Jefferson Hardin was the only African American to serve in the Wyoming territorial legislature. He served two terms, first in 1879 and again in 1882.

Hardin lived in Kentucky until around 1850, when he traveled to California to prospect for gold. Finding no luck in the goldfields, he traveled for a while and then joined the Union army in 1862. Finding racial tensions within his regiment, he left in 1863 and headed west to Colorado.

Hardin became known for his speaking skills, and he advocated for equal rights for blacks and supported public school integration and black suffrage. He was named delegate-at-large from Colorado Territory to the Republican National Convention in 1872.

For various reasons, Hardin and his wife, Nellie, moved in 1873 to Cheyenne, Wyoming, where he opened a barbershop. He gained recognition in Wyoming as a fine speaker and was elected to represent Laramie County in the territorial legislative assembly in 1879 and in 1882.

During his first term, Hardin introduced bills to protect dairymen and to protect poultry. The poultry bill set a twenty-five-cent bounty on chicken hawks and eagles. He also served on the Indian and Military Affairs Committees. During the 1882 assembly, Hardin sponsored a bill that expanded the city boundaries of Cheyenne and a bill that made it a misdemeanor to use weapons in a threatening manner except in cases of self-defense.

In 1882, the Hardins moved to Utah. He also operated barbershops in that state and was active in politics. He died in 1889.[45]

WYOMING'S FIRST
BLACK WOMAN LEGISLATOR

Harriet Elizabeth Byrd

Harriet Elizabeth "Liz" Byrd was the first black woman to serve in the Wyoming House of Representatives, from 1981 to 1988, and in the Wyoming Senate, from 1989 to 1992. *Wyoming State Archives, Department of State Parks and Cultural Resources.*

Wyoming's first black woman legislator, known as "Liz" Byrd, served in the Wyoming House of Representatives from 1981 to 1988. She was also the first African American to serve in the Wyoming Senate, where she was seated from 1989 to 1992.

Born in Wyoming in 1926, Liz was the granddaughter of Charles Rhone, who had come to Wyoming Territory in 1876 and worked for the railroad and as a cowboy. Liz graduated from Cheyenne High School in 1944 but was not accepted as a student at the University of Wyoming (probably because of her race). She instead attended West Virginia State College.

While visiting in Cheyenne in 1946, Liz attempted to make a purchase at F.E. Warren Air Force Base but was unable to do so because she did not have a military identification card. The soldier waiting behind her in line, James Byrd, helped her, and they became friends and married a year later. James Byrd joined the Cheyenne Police Department after his service in the military. He eventually became the first black chief of police in Cheyenne and in Wyoming. He served for sixteen years and was also appointed U.S. marshal for the Wyoming District.

Liz earned a degree in elementary education in 1949 but was unable to secure a job teaching in Laramie County (probably because of her race). She worked as a post supply administrator at F.E. Warren Air Force Base and taught classes for the Technical Training Wing there for a decade. In 1959, Liz Byrd was at last hired by the Laramie County School District. She taught mostly second-graders but also fourth and fifth grades. She also served on various committees throughout the school system.

Liz Byrd's concern about the lack of benefits for teachers and inadequate teaching materials led to her desire to run for elected office. Her son James

A mounted bison once stood in the rotunda of the capitol and is now at the Wyoming State Museum. Representative Liz Byrd, with the assistance of Wyoming's fourth-grade students, introduced a bill to name the bison Wyoming's state mammal. *Starley Talbott photograph.*

said that when she campaigned, she went to every event possible and went door-to-door to talk with her constituents.

During her terms in the Wyoming House of Representatives and Senate, she worked for laws for adequate handicapped parking, for the creation of social services for adults and for a child seatbelt law, in addition to her actions for teachers and students. She was the primary sponsor of the Martin Luther King Holiday Bill, bringing it before the Wyoming legislature nine times. There was much controversy over the bill, but it was finally passed in 1990 with a compromise to add the words "equality day" to the final bill. She also sponsored the bill to name the American bison as Wyoming's state animal with the assistance of fourth-grade students from Wyoming schools.

Liz Byrd retired from teaching in 1996 and was honored in 2012 as a distinguished alumna by the University of Wyoming. The University of Wyoming African American and Diaspora Studies Department also created a speaker series named for her, stating that Liz Byrd is emblematic of what we all hope to accomplish in life and that she has made lives better in the state of Wyoming.

Her son James became a member of the Wyoming House of Representatives in 2008 and said of his mother, "It would be impossible given the political climate of today to replicate her achievements. What I do embrace is the same set of social values and standards of excellence in my work."

Upon the death of Liz Byrd on January 27, 2015, at the age of eighty-eight, Governor Matt Mead said, "She was a role model for all people, for women and for Wyoming."[46]

WYOMING'S FIRST FULL-TERM WOMAN SPEAKER OF THE HOUSE

Verda James

Verda James, born in 1901, moved to Wyoming when she became a teacher at Natrona County High School in Casper. She had earned her undergraduate degree from the University of Iowa and her master's degree from the University of Denver.

In 1939, James began working for the Wyoming Department of Education, eventually becoming director of the Special Education Division. She also served as the state's deputy director of public instruction and was instrumental in creating remedial reading programs. In 1955, she joined the Casper College faculty, teaching English and education. She became assistant superintendent for elementary education for Natrona County School District in 1958.

Verda's interest in helping children led to her serving eight terms, from 1954 to 1970, in the Wyoming House of Representatives. She

Verda James served eight terms in the Wyoming House of Representatives and was the first full-time woman Speaker of the House from 1969 to 1970. *Wyoming State Archives, Department of State Parks and Cultural Resources.*

chaired the House Education Committee for three terms and was the only Republican woman in the house during most of that time. James served on the Governor's Committee on Education and the Status of Women. She was the first woman to serve a full term as Speaker of the Wyoming House of Representatives in 1969–1970.

James was not the first woman to ever hold the position of Speaker of the House—Edness Kimball Wilkins was serving as majority leader in the house when Speaker Walter Phelan died in office. After Phelan's death, Wilkins was promoted to speaker in May 1966. However, Wilkins ran successfully for the state senate in the fall, so she served as Speaker for only a short time.

James was honored with the naming of Verda James Elementary School in Casper. She died in Casper on October 15, 1991.[47]

FIRST WOMAN ELECTED TO STATEWIDE OFFICE IN WYOMING

Estelle Reel

Estelle Reel accepted a job to teach school in Cheyenne, Wyoming, in 1886. She had been educated in Boston, St. Louis and Chicago. Some school board members criticized her actions outside of the classroom, but she quickly let them know they had no right to dictate where she went to church, bought her clothes or boarded.

The voters seemed to approve of Estelle, and they elected her as the school superintendent of Laramie County in 1890. She was re-elected two years later, after which she sought to become the state superintendent of schools in 1894. The state superintendent of public instruction is one of five executive officers elected by Wyoming voters. The other four are governor, secretary of state, state auditor and state treasurer.

After securing the nomination for the state office, Estelle worked hard on the campaign trail. She traveled throughout the state by railroad, stagecoach, ranch wagon and horseback. She was described as an attractive woman who sported a pompadour hairstyle with a bun. Estelle charmed audiences with a short stump speech that focused on the state's great potential for economic growth. Critics argued that she wouldn't be able to handle the complex duties of the superintendent as well as being the secretary of the state land board. The *Carbon County Journal* said she would be "Putty in the hands of the Cheyenne ring. The only safe thing to do is defeat her with the rest of the gang ticket."

Estelle Reel was the first woman to serve as the Wyoming state superintendent of public instruction in 1894 and was national superintendent of Indian schools from 1897 to 1910. *Wyoming State Archives, Department of State Parks and Cultural Resources.*

Reel won handily by carrying every county in Wyoming. She became the first woman Wyoming voters ever elected to a statewide office. Her detractors said she had won because she enclosed her picture in perfumed letters sent to lonely cowboys, who were so smitten they rode more than one hundred miles to vote for her and waved guns in the faces of those who dared to vote against her.

The new superintendent quickly proved that she could handle the complexities of her office. The revenue for schools depended on how much was collected from ranchers who bought or leased land that had been set aside as state public school sections. She made changes to the state's system of investing the interest from the funds, thereby increasing the revenue for schools.

Reel supported a standardized curriculum, the free distribution of textbooks and teacher certification. Little progress was made on these matters during her tenure, however. After three years, she decided to leave her post as the Wyoming state superintendent to become the national superintendent of Indian schools in Washington, D.C.

As superintendent of Indian schools, Reel was in charge of 250 Indian schools in the United States with a combined enrollment of about twenty thousand students. The work required Reel to spend a good deal of time traveling. In her first two years in office, she traveled more than forty-one thousand miles to visit 49 Indian schools. About two thousand of those miles were by wagon, packhorse or on foot.

In consensus with the views of her time, Superintendent Reel focused on the dignity of labor for Indian students. She thought that Indian students who were going to be servants or agricultural laborers required a practical education that didn't raise their standards or expectations to unreasonable levels. She did recognize the importance to the economy provided by the skills of Indian women in the fields of basketry, sewing, netting, reed work and weaving and promoted the cultural importance of retaining those skills.

Estelle Reel held the position as Indian superintendent until 1910, when she resigned to marry Cort Meyer, a Washington farmer and rancher. She moved to Washington State, never again ran for public office, and died in 1959 at the age of ninety-seven.[48]

During the 2018 session of the Wyoming legislature, a bill was enacted providing for the recognition of Estelle Reel as the first woman elected to hold the office of state superintendent of public instruction in Wyoming and the second woman elected to hold a statewide office anywhere in the United States. The bill designated January 7 of each year as Estelle Reel Day, to be observed by state and local governments. The date may also be observed in the public schools and by organizations within the state.[49]

THE FIRST WOMAN IN WYOMING ELECTED AS SECRETARY OF STATE

Thyra Thomson

Republican Thyra Thomson, widow of a popular Wyoming politician, U.S. representative Keith Thomson, was able to transfer her late husband's popularity into a victory when she was elected Wyoming's secretary of state in 1963. She was the first woman elected to that office, and she served five terms, retiring in 1987.

Often referred to as the "Queen of Wyoming," sort of a cross between a Broadway star and a Wyoming cowgirl, Thyra was known for speaking up for her citizens' needs and concerns. She led efforts for equal pay for women and recognition of the comparable worth of women's jobs, and she advocated for adequate and affordable daycare. Thomson also worked in areas of finance and supported efforts for investors to have a fair balance between risk and reward.

Thyra Thomson served on many state, national and international committees. In 1974, she was elected president of the North American Securities Administrators, encompassing the fifty states, ten Canadian provinces and Mexico. She served on the Unesco Youth Committee and on the Health, Education and Welfare Allied Health Professional Council.

Thomson traveled the world to promote Wyoming products. She worked on trade relations with China, Saudi Arabia, Jordan, Egypt, France and South America. Thyra was instrumental in China's purchase of the state

Thyra Thomson was the first woman to be elected as Wyoming's secretary of state. She served five terms from 1963 to 1987. *Wyoming State Archives, Department of State Parks and Cultural Resources.*

of Wyoming's entire wheat crop in 1984. In 1985, she was a delegate to the North and South American Securities Conference in Colombia, and in 1986, she was a delegate to the International Securities Conference in Paris.

Thyra was also known for her charitable work and for her great sense of humor. A favorite anecdote about Thyra was quoted by author Kerry Drake: "She was at a fundraiser for a Learning Center for developmentally disabled children in Cheyenne, and she agreed to shine the shoes of the man who was the highest bidder." The man who won the bid paid $32.50, and Thomson said that she got down on her knees and shined his shoes by the Esther Hobart Morris statue (Morris was a leader of Wyoming's women's suffrage movement) in front of the Wyoming Capitol. When asked why she participated in such a stunt, Thyra replied, "I raised money for charity, didn't I, and he had a good time."[50]

Upon Thomson's death on June 11, 2013, at the age of ninety-six, she was remembered fondly. Max Maxfield, then Wyoming secretary of state, said,

Wyoming has lost a legendary Wyoming public servant and a vanguard of her time with the passing of Thyra Thomson. Her contributions to her beloved State are immeasurable and significant in the legacy she leaves us all. During her historic 24 years, as Wyoming's Secretary of State, she touched the lives of citizens throughout the State. Through her dedicated service and statesmanship, Thyra Thomson earned a well-deserved and iconic place in Wyoming's history.[51]

STATUES, ART AND SYMBOLS

STATUES

Esther Hobart Morris

Though several statues grace the grounds of the Wyoming State Capitol, none are as prominent, have caused as much controversy or been celebrated as much as the memorial to Esther Hobart Morris. A replica of the statue located in Statuary Hall in Washington, D.C., the Wyoming Capitol's statue of Esther Hobart Morris honors her advocacy for women's suffrage and her service as the first woman justice of the peace in South Pass City, Wyoming, in 1870.

Wyoming was at the forefront of the women's suffrage movement. The first victory for women's suffrage in the United States occurred when the territorial legislature of Wyoming passed a bill granting women the right to vote in 1869. When Wyoming applied for admission to the Union in 1889, arguments ensued in Washington over Wyoming's policy of women's suffrage, and chances for statehood seemed in question. Joseph M. Carey, the territorial delegate in Washington, telegraphed the Wyoming legislature that women's suffrage may have to be abandoned to gain statehood. The legislature responded, "We will remain out of the Union a hundred years rather than come in without the women."[52]

Even though Esther Hobart Morris is credited with being a major factor in advocating for and introducing the women's suffrage bill in the territorial

The statue of Esther Hobart Morris on the grounds of the Wyoming Capitol. *Starley Talbott photograph.*

legislature in 1869, contemporary historians believe she played a minor role in the bill's introduction.

Many people have written articles and books attempting to explain why women's suffrage first took root in Wyoming. A vast majority of these works cite the contributions of two South Pass City residents, William H. Bright and Esther H. Morris. According to the story, Morris held a tea party in her home in South Pass City in September 1869 for forty members of the community. During the tea party, Morris received a promise from William Bright and Herman Nickerson, both candidates for Wyoming's first territorial council, that whichever man won, he would introduce a suffrage bill in the council. Bright, the Democrat, won, and he introduced the bill, which passed and was signed by Governor John Campbell.

It has been debated over the years if there was ever actually a tea party hosted by Morris in her South Pass home, which was quite small and probably could not have held forty people. Moreover, there were nine candidates for the council, not just Bright and Nickerson. Most contemporary historians give William Bright the major credit for introducing the women's suffrage bill.[53]

A January 18, 1870 letter published in the *Revolution*, a woman suffrage publication, explains what may have happened. The letter, written by Robert Morris, Esther's youngest son, and dated December 27, 1869, states:

> *Mr. Bright returned to his home in this place a few days ago, and Mrs. Morris and myself, as the only open advocates here of Woman's Suffrage, resolved ourselves into a committee, and called on him to render our congratulations and thanks for his services in our behalf as well as for all true lovers of Equal Rights.*
>
> *We found Mr. Bright in a comfortable log cabin with his good wife and little son. We met with a cordial reception and he expressed himself pleased that there were some persons here who endorsed his views on Woman Suffrage.*
>
> *Mr. Bright told us, "I have never thought much about it, nor have I been converted by a woman's lecture or newspaper, for I have never heard a woman speak from the podium and never read The Revolution. I knew that it was a new issue, and a live one, and with a strong feeling that it was just, I determined to use all my influence in my power to have the bill passed."*

When the first territorial legislative session commenced on October 12, 1869, William Bright was elected as the council president. Later in the session, Bright introduced the women's suffrage bill. Historians relate that he personally believed in women's suffrage for a variety of reasons. Since the nation would not repeal black suffrage, which he adamantly opposed, he reasoned that white women should also vote, since they were socially and intellectually superior to the former slaves. Bright had openly stated that if blacks were allowed to vote, then his mother and wife should be permitted to cast ballots.[54]

The bill was debated and amended several times but passed in the legislature and was signed into law on December 10, 1869, reading as follows:

> *Be it enacted by the Council and House of Representatives of the Territory of Wyoming: Section 1. That every woman of the age of twenty-one years, residing in this territory, may at every election to be holden under the laws thereof, cast her vote. And her rights to the elective franchise and to hold office shall be the same under the election laws of the territory, as those of electors. Sec. 2. This act shall take effect and be in force from and after its passage.*

As for Esther Hobart Morris, she became a national figure in the women's suffrage movement because of her appointment as a justice of the peace at South Pass City beginning in February 1870. She served for eight and one half months and heard twenty-seven cases. Most of her cases were disagreements over debts, although ten cases involved assaults.[55]

Morris declined to seek election for justice of the peace, though she stated that holding the job had demonstrated that women could perform well in elected offices. In a letter to those attending a suffrage convention in January 1871 in Washington, D.C., Morris wrote the following:

> So far as woman suffrage has progressed in this Territory, we are entirely indebted to men. To William H. Bright belongs the honor of presenting the woman suffrage bill; and it was our district Judge, Hon. John W. Kingham, who proposed my appointment as a justice of the peace and the trial of women as jurors.
>
> Circumstances have transpired to make my position as a Justice of the Peace a test of woman's ability to hold public office, and I feel that my work has been satisfactory, although I have often regretted I was not better qualified to fill the position. Like all pioneers, I have labored more in faith and hope.
>
> I have assisted in drawing a grand and petit jury, deposited a ballot, and helped canvass the votes after election, and in performing all these duties I do not know as I have neglected my family any more than in ordinary shopping, and I must admit that I have been better paid for the services rendered than for any I have ever performed. In some thirty civil actions, tried before me, there has been not one appeal taken, and the judgement was affirmed in the court above, and in the criminal cases also before me there has been no call for a jury.
>
> My idea of the woman question in Wyoming is, that while we enjoy the privilege of the elective franchise, we have not been sufficiently educated up to it. The election here, and agitation of woman's voting has caused us to think and has placed us far in advance of what we were, and I now think that we shall be able to sustain the position which has been granted to us.

Wyoming went on to become the forty-fourth state admitted to the Union and retained women's suffrage rights within the state's constitution. The Wyoming State Capitol is a national historic landmark not because of its architecture but because of its history. The inclusion of women's sufferage in Wyoming's constitution made it unique in U.S. history.[56]

Chief Washakie

The statue of Chief Washakie on the grounds of the Wyoming Capitol. *Starley Talbott photograph.*

Another statue of great importance to Wyoming is that of the Shoshone chief Washakie. The Wyoming Capitol's memorial, as well as the statue of Chief Washakie in Statuary Hall in Washington, D.C., depicts the importance of Native Americans in Wyoming. Chief Washakie, as an influential leader of the Shoshone people, advocated for peace rather than war, and he was considered to be a great friend of the white people. He was believed to have been born around 1800, lived for a century, and died on February 20, 1900.[57]

When Chief Washakie died in 1900 on the Wind River Indian Reservation in Wyoming, he was memorialized by the camp commander with these words:

His countenance was one of rugged strength mingled with kindness.... Washakie was a great man, for he was a brave man and a good man. The spirit of his loyalty and courage will speak to soldiers; the memory of his love for his own people will linger to assist them in their troubles, and he will never be forgotten so long as the mountains and streams of Wyoming, which were his home, bear his name.[58]

The statement on Washakie's statue at the Wyoming Capitol, sculpted by Dave McGary, reads, "Chief Washakie stood for bravery and courage. He was a peacemaker, a strong leader and above all a wise and generous man."

Other Statues

The capitol grounds also contain a statue dedicated to those who participated in the Spanish-American War and a replica of the Liberty Bell. John W. Snyder, secretary of the treasury under President Harry S. Truman, presented the bell to the people of Wyoming as an inspirational symbol of the U.S. Bond Independence Drive, which occurred in 1950.

Sculptor Edward J. Fraughton conceived a symbol representing the state in his *The Spirit of Wyoming*, a statue placed within the Capitol Square in 1986. It depicts the struggles of animal and man against nature and time, and it is a tribute praising people of the past, present and future. Also on the capitol grounds is a handsome bronze statue of a bison sculpted by Cheyenne artist Dan Ostermiller and made possible by donations from Wyoming citizens.

A wrought-iron fence once surrounded the capitol building and lawns. The fence was removed at some point in time, and the grounds now contain a number of trees indigenous to Wyoming.

ART

Within the capitol are many works of art symbolizing the history of Wyoming and especially depicting frontier and pioneer life in the West. The west wing's second and third stories are occupied by the senate chamber, gallery, lobbies and anterooms. The east wing is similarly designed for the house of representatives. Each chamber's ceiling contains a large section of stained glass into which are set emblems of the Great Seal of the State of Wyoming.

On the walls of the senate and house chambers hang a number of paintings, among which are several by the famous Western artist William Gollings. The paintings by Gollings in the senate chamber are entitled *The Smoke Signal* and *The Wagon Box Fight*. The house chamber includes paintings titled *Emigrants on the Platte* and *Overland Stage*.[59]

Artist William "Bill" Gollings, born in 1878, came to Wyoming at the age of twenty and worked as a ranch hand and cowboy. He worked for five years branding cattle, driving a stagecoach, trapping for fur and hunting for gold. His artwork showcased what he experienced in his life on the Wyoming range.[60]

Gollings later studied at the Chicago Academy of Fine Arts, and he then returned to Wyoming to settle in Sheridan and open an art studio in 1909. He spent the rest of his life as an artist and stated in February 1923:

> *In the early spring 1903 I sent to Montgomery Ward & Company for some oil colors and other equipment to paint with. When the snow went off I made a few crude attempts at picture-making. The people on the ranch where I stayed and called home thought them wonderful. That summer I covered the mess tent with charcoal studies; horse heads and certain characters who interested and asked my brother to bring me over. I built a shack and called it a studio. The skylight in the roof gave me the right to call it such. I had*

met and talked with a few of America's foremost painters: H.H. Sharp, Howard Russell Butler, William B. Henderson, C.M. Russell, Frederic Remington and a few lesser lights. They have all had a good influence on my work. My work has had a good distribution throughout the United States and even in foreign countries. Four of my pictures are in the Wyoming Capitol at Cheyenne: "The Smoke Signal, Indian Attack on the Overland Stage, Emigrants on the Platte, and The Wagon Box Fight." I have no pictures in permanent galleries. I do not consider the others worth mentioning. Work for the rest of my life is ahead of me with only one thing that would ever take me from it; to be younger and have the country open and unsettled as it was when I first made riding my profession.[61]

Eight murals, four in each chamber of the Wyoming Capitol, were painted by Allen Tupper True, a noted Western artist and Colorado native. His murals have graced three U.S. capitols—in Colorado, Wyoming and Missouri. True was an authority on Western cowboy gear, life and culture and on Native American life, culture and design. His Wyoming murals depict pioneer life in Wyoming and are titled *Indian Chief Cheyenne, Frontier Cavalry Officers, Pony Express Rider, Railroad Builders-Surveyors, Cattlemen, Trappers, Homesteaders* and *Stagecoach.*[62]

Allen Tupper True's vision of the Western venture and peoples he so admired and revered is vividly brought to life in a biography describing his art. He is said to have painted a way of life "that streaked across the American land and psyche like a shooting star: bright, brief, and unique." A biography of the artist traces his life from his earliest beginnings in Colorado and describes his artistic evolution as an illustrator, an easel painter and a muralist. Written by True's daughter Jere and his granddaughter Victoria, the work is a personal memoir of Allen True's life and work.[63]

A letter from Allen Tupper True and a segment from the contract depict the proposal by the artist to the Capitol Commission as follows:

February 9, 1917
Capitol Commission, State of Wyoming, Cheyenne, Wyoming

Gentlemen:

In pursuance of your request I present herewith my proposal for mural decorations for the Chambers of the Senate and House of Representatives of the State Capitol.

In the Senate Chamber to paint and install four mural decorations in the panels of the second floor, $500.00 each or $2,000.00 for the set. These paintings to represent pioneer types through the portraiture of typical prominent men of early Wyoming history and to accord with sketches to be submitted to the Commission.

In the House of Representatives, to paint and install four mural paintings in the panels on the second floor, $800.00 each or $3200.00 for the set. These paintings to represent phases of the life of the early builders of Wyoming, such as the Miners, the Trappers, the Homesteaders and the Cattlemen, and to conform with sketches previously approved by the Capitol Commission.

In connection with this proposal I submit some extracts from newspaper comment on my work and photographs of some of my mural paintings in other public buildings, which serve to indicate the type of work contemplated.

At a time when public buildings in the country are being much decorated with mural paintings of an allegorical type, there is a fine opportunity here in Wyoming to use the magnificent historical data of the State for subject matter; to honor the pioneer and to record for coming generations the picturesque phases of the West, which were nowhere more adaptable than in Wyoming. This I propose to do.

Very respectfully,
Allen T. True

A portion of the contract and agreement between Allen True and the Capitol Building Commission reads as follows:

By this contract, entered into this 27th day of August, A.D. 1917, in the City of Cheyenne, State of Wyoming, it is mutually agreed and understood by and between Allen True of Denver, Colorado, party of the first part, and the Capitol Building Commission of the State of Wyoming, party of the second part:

That the party of the first part shall paint four (4) mural decorations for designated panels in the Senate Chamber of the Wyoming State Capitol, and four (4) mural decorations for designated panels in the chamber of the House of Representatives, said mural decorations shall accord with and amplify the eight sketches previously approved by the party of the second part: That the party of the first part shall assume the expense of the placing of the murals in position, and repair any attendant damage *to surrounding structure or surfaces in a thorough and workmanlike manner….The total and complete sum of all payments to be fifty-two hundred ($5,200.) dollars.*[64]

A mural by Powell, Wyoming artist Mike Kopriva titled *Wyoming, the Land, the People* was unveiled in 1982. The painting depicts Wyoming's culture and lifestyles, past and present. In the lower left corner of the painting is a hidden picture of Wyoming's only three-term governor, Ed Herschler.

A number of other paintings may be found throughout the capitol, including individual photographs of members of the legislature and elected officials. Other artwork can be found painted on the walls in the form of border decorations, much of which was covered over by former remodeling projects and is now visible through the restoration work of the latest capitol renovation.

One photographic collage, hanging in the third-floor lobby of the house of representatives, attests to a tumultuous era within the house of state. The collage, a composite of all the Democratic Party legislators of 1913, shows a tear in the paper that cuts across the face of T.C. Diers, a banker from Sheridan. The legend tells of a practically knock-down fight between Republicans and Democrats over who should sit in the Speaker of the House chair. The story goes that the twelfth session of the legislature convened in January 1913 with high stakes over which party would gain power over the house. At that time, voters did not directly elect senators, leaving that duty to the legislature. The two leading candidates were Republican F.E. Warren and Democrat John B. Kendrick.[65]

In the 1913 legislative session, Wyoming's fifty-seven-member house consisted of twenty-nine Republicans and twenty-eight Democrats. Martin Luther Pratt, a Republican merchant from Powell, decided he would not caucus with the Republicans and would run for Speaker of the House. Pratt and one other Republican joined the Democrats, giving them the majority and giving Pratt the speakership. The Democrats would thus decide who would be the senator from Wyoming.

According to a report from the *Wyoming Tribune* newspaper, during the second week of the session, Pratt left the speaker's chair to debate from the floor. The Democrat Speaker Pro Tem, William Wood, then sat in the Speaker's chair and called for a vote from the elections committee. Pratt claimed Wood was out of order in calling for the vote and demanded Wood leave the chair. When Wood refused and again called for a vote, Pratt sprang to the platform and shoved Wood to the side. Other members of the house entered the fracas, which reportedly lasted for nearly an hour and resulted in the smashing of the photographic collage over the head of one of the delegates. Finally a truce was called, and the house adjourned until the following day. A few days later, the lawmakers voted to retain F.E. Warren in his seat in the U.S. Senate.[66]

Symbols

Within the capitol, the main attraction is the central portion of the building, the rotunda, consisting of a circular hall thirty feet in diameter and fifty-four feet in height from floor to the stained-glass dome above. Above the stained glass, and not visible from the floor below, is the airy lantern, which allows light to penetrate the stained glass.

The capitol rotunda once held a mounted life-size elk and an American bison. In 1985, at the urging of Wyoming's fourth-grade students and under

A view of the stained-glass dome above the center of the capitol rotunda from the floor of the rotunda. *J.E. Stimson Collection, Wyoming State Archives, Department of State Parks and Cultural Resources.*

the guidance of Representative Harriet "Liz" Byrd, the state legislature designated the American bison as Wyoming's state mammal. The mounted animals are now housed in the collections of the Wyoming State Museum.

Wyoming is known as the Cowboy State and the Equality State. The state motto is Equal Rights.

The Wyoming state flag was designed by Verna Keyes of Casper and was adopted by the fourteenth legislature on January 31, 1917. The Great Seal of Wyoming is the heart of the flag and is imprinted on the bison. The bison was once the monarch of the plains. The colors of the state flag are red, white and blue. The red border represents the Indian and the blood of the pioneers who gave their lives reclaiming the soil. White is the emblem of purity and uprightness over Wyoming. Blue, the color of the sky and mountains, is symbolic of fidelity, justice and virility.

The Great Seal of the State of Wyoming was adopted by the second legislature in 1893 and revised by the sixteenth legislature in 1921. The two dates on the Great Seal, 1869 and 1890, commemorate the organization of the territorial government and Wyoming's admission to the Union. The draped figure in the center holds a staff from which flows a banner bearing the words "Equal Rights" and symbolizes the political status women have always enjoyed in Wyoming. The male figures typify the livestock and mining industries of the state. The number 44 on the five-pointed star signifies that Wyoming was the forty-fourth state admitted to the Union. On top of the pillars rest lamps from which burn the light of knowledge. Scrolls encircling the two pillars bear the words Oil, Mines, Livestock and Grain, four of Wyoming's major industries.

The state flower is the Indian paintbrush, adopted January 31, 1917. The bison was adopted as the state mammal on February 23, 1985. The state bird is the meadowlark, adopted February 6, 1927. The state tree is the plains cottonwood, adopted in 1947 and amended in 1961. The state gemstone is jade, adopted in 1967. The state fish is the cutthroat trout, adopted in 1987. The state reptile is the horned toad, adopted in 1993. The state fossil is knightia, adopted in 1987. The state dinosaur is the triceratops, adopted in 1994. Other symbols include the state sport of rodeo, adopted in 2003; the state grass, western wheatgrass, adopted in 2007; and the state insect, Sheridan's green hairstreak butterfly, adopted in 2009. The state coin is the Sacajawea golden dollar, adopted in 2004. Sacajawea was a Shoshone woman who accompanied and assisted the Lewis and Clark Expedition in its exploration of the Western United States. The coin depicts Sacagawea and her son, Jean Baptiste.

The Wyoming state seal is depicted in stained glass on the ceiling of the senate chamber. *Starley Talbott photograph.*

The state license plate is unique because it features an iconic bucking horse and rider. In 1935, Secretary of State Lester Hunt proposed legislation to make changes to the Wyoming license plate design. He commissioned Allen Tupper True to design the new plate, which was first used in 1936. The bucking horse and rider is the registered trademark of Wyoming.

In 2010, the state code, known as the "Code of the West," was adopted. The state legislature derived the code from the book *Cowboy Ethics* by James P. Owens and included these ten points of conduct: 1. Live each day with courage; 2. Take pride in your work; 3. Always finish what you start; 4. Do what has to be done; 5. Be tough but fair; 6. When you make a promise, keep it; 7. Ride for the brand; 8. Talk less, say more; 9. Remember that some things are not for sale; and 10. Know where to draw the line.

The state song, "Wyoming," was composed by C.E. Winter (lyrics) and G.E. Knapp (music) and was adopted in 1955 with the following words:

I

In the far and mighty West
Where the crimson sun seeks rest,
There's a growing splendid state that lies above,
On the breast of this great land,
Where the massive Rockies stand,
There's Wyoming young and strong, the state I love!
Chorus
Wyoming, Wyoming! Land of the sunlight clear!
Wyoming, Wyoming! Land that we hold so dear!
Wyoming, Wyoming! Precious art thou and thine!
Wyoming, Wyoming! Beloved state of mine!

II

In the flowers wild and sweet
Colors rare and perfumes meet,
There's the columbine so pure, the daisy too,
Wild the rose and red it springs,
White the button and its rings,
Thou are loyal for they're red and white and blue.

III

Where thy peaks with crowned head,
Rising till the sky they wed,
Sit like snow queens ruling wood and stream and plain;
'Neath thy bosom's broadened sweep,
Lie the riches that have gained and brought thee fame.

IV

Other treasure thou dost hold,
Men and women thou dost mould,
True and earnest are the lives that thou dost raise,
Strength thy children thou dost teach,
Nature's truth thou givest to each
Free and noble are they workings and thy ways.

The Wyoming Capitol Building in winter. *Wyoming State Archives, Department of State Parks and Cultural Resources.*

V
In the nation's banner free
There's one star that has for me
A radiance pure and splendor like the sun;
Mine it is, Wyoming's star
Home it leads me near or far;
O Wyoming! All my heart and love you've won!

6

CHANGES TO THE CAPITOL SQUARE

T he Wyoming Capitol, located just north of the geographical center of Cheyenne, is a dominant structure on the city skyline. The building is complementary to the Union Pacific Depot ten blocks south—the two buildings are on opposite ends of a north–south axis formed by Capitol Avenue.

At one time, parks were located adjacent to the depot and the capitol. The impressive locations were described in the July 23, 1890 edition of the *Cheyenne Daily Leader*:

> *In all Cheyenne, which is preeminently a city of handsome buildings, no structure compares in massiveness and beauty with Wyoming's statehouse, a noble structure at the head of Capitol Avenue. At the foot of this broad, tree fringed thoroughfare is the splendid Union Pacific passenger depot, an edifice in character essentially a cross match companion piece to the palace like home of the rulers of the young commonwealth.*
>
> *Immediately in front of the statehouse is the beautiful city park aptly described as the municipal pleasure ground. It is a healthy young forest with lawns dotted with flower beds and provided with other adjuncts which challenge the admiration of the visitor posted in the Capitol. The Capitol surroundings contribute in no small degree to its attractiveness.*

The landscaping of the capitol grounds has changed over time. The earliest views of the capitol indicate that landscaping was not undertaken during the period when the building was being expanded. Foundation plantings were minimal. An iron fence that enclosed the grounds was the major landscape feature.

Street trees were planted between the sidewalk and the street. These trees were closely spaced along the south edge of the capitol building block. By the late 1920s, the iron fence had been removed, and some foundation plantings were present. Concrete benches flanking the main entrance appeared in the 1920s. During the 1940s, flowerbeds extended to the east and west of the benches.

Since those early Cheyenne days, the two parks south of the capitol have been displaced by buildings. Trees no longer line Capitol Avenue, and several buildings were removed from that thoroughfare. Yet despite the changes, Capitol Avenue remains a major transportation artery.

The capitol is situated on approximately three quarters of an acre. It is part of a fourteen-acre state government complex of buildings including the Barret Building, housing the Wyoming State Museum, the Wyoming

The capitol around 1905 as photographed by Joseph Stimson, who was employed as a photographer for the Union Pacific Railroad and was a prolific freelance photographer. *J.E. Stimson Collection, Wyoming State Archives, Department of State Parks and Cultural Resources.*

Joseph Stimson's house, pictured around 1905, was located just north of the capitol. Stimson was a noted photographer of the time and provided thousands of photographs depicting locations and scenes throughout Wyoming. *J.E. Stimson Collection, Wyoming State Archives, Department of State Parks and Cultural Resources.*

State Archives and the office of the Wyoming State Parks and Historic Sites. Other buildings include the Wyoming State Supreme Court building, the Hathaway Office Building and the Herschler Office Building.

The present-day area constituting Capitol Square includes the capitol and the Herschler Building to the north of the capitol. The Herschler Building was constructed in 1981–83 at a cost of $27.3 million and is named after former governor Ed Herschler. Office space for state agencies, underground parking and underground access are the features.

The Herschler Building underwent major changes in conjunction with the 2018–19 renovations at the capitol. The original building included an atrium that was removed during the current project. Removal of the atrium allows more light to enter the offices, and the views of the capitol from the north side of Capitol Avenue are now restored.

The original design of the Herschler Building featured two wings. A new first-floor lobby and a new elevator were installed in the center of the building to connect the two wings. New entryways were added on the north and south sides of the center of each wing to provide more efficient access into the building and to elevators and restrooms. The mechanical distribution system has been replaced, along with lighting and electrical systems. Restrooms were remodeled and expanded, and plumbing was replaced. Ceilings, carpet and paint were updated.

The exterior of the Herschler Building was replaced to address major maintenance issues, including water infiltration, corrosion, wall gaps and rotting window blocks. The new exterior relates to the scale of the capitol and is complimentary to it. Replacing some aspects of the exterior provided the opportunity to expand the building toward the south.

Original windowless south-facing walls of the Herschler Building have been replaced with offices containing windows that overlook the capitol. The added space allowed for meeting rooms for staff, legislative committees and legislative session staff.

A concrete plaza once graced the space between the capitol and the Herschler Building. Most of the plaza has been converted to a parklike

The Herschler Office Building as it underwent updating and renovation from 2017 to 2019. *Starley Talbott photograph.*

setting. An underground passageway connects the Herschler Building to the capitol. The roof of the passage was replaced with skylights, allowing more light to enter the area. The passageway was also expanded, and plans included adding public spaces such as additional meeting rooms, an auditorium and a student learning center. Some of those amenities were contingent on the availability of funds near the end of the project and may be completed at a later time.[67]

The renovation of the capitol as part of the Capitol Square Project is discussed in Chapter 7.

7

PRESERVING THE HERITAGE

For more than 125 years, the Wyoming Capitol has stood as a symbol of the spirit of the people of Wyoming. Through struggles mighty and small, the state has persevered and thrived. Many additions, updates and improvements have been made to the physical building.

The Wyoming legislature approved the major Capitol Building Project for a complete renovation of the capitol and adjacent office buildings in 2015 at a cost of approximately $219 million. An additional $80 million was allocated for furnishings, equipment, design services, temporary office space for relocation during construction and a contingency fund to address unanticipated needs. The capitol was closed in 2016, and the grand reopening celebration was slated for July 2019.

The State of Wyoming served as the project owner of the Capitol Building Project. For contract purposes, the Oversight Group on Capitol Rehabilitation and Restoration was named as the project owner. The Oversight Group was created in 2014 and comprised the governor and eight members of the legislature. The Advisory Task Force on Capitol Building Rehabilitation and Restoration provided advice and recommendations to the Oversight Group. Paul Brown, as the agent of MOCA Systems, served as the project owner's representative for the Capitol Square Project. Wyoming State Parks and Cultural Resources, with Sara Needles as the cultural resources division administrator, served in an advisory capacity, offering input on matters of historic preservation. HDR Inc. was the architect of record for the project and was responsible for design. Michael

Ezra Meeker and Governor Bryant Brooks with a wagon and team in front of the capitol around 1910, depicting an early-day scene typical of the Western culture of Wyoming. *Wyoming State Archives, Department of State Parks and Cultural Resources.*

Dixon of HDR was the onsite preservation architect. Wendy Madsen served as special projects manager, and the company of J.E. Dunn was the construction manager of risk and was responsible for construction.[68]

The Capitol Square Project comprised four interrelated components: rehabilitation and restoration of the capitol; replacement, relocation and expansion of the central utility plant; remodeling and expansion of the underground passageway that connects the capitol to the Herschler Building; and rehabilitation and expansion of the Herschler Building. The underground passageway between the capitol and the Herschler Building was expanded underneath the Herschler Building to extend nearly to Twenty-Sixth Street.

The 129-year-old capitol building was in dire need of upgrades to meet safety standards and modern technology issues. There were few smoke detectors and no smoke evacuation or fire suppression systems. Fire and smoke could have spread quickly throughout the building, and occupants would have had only a few minutes to evacuate safely. Many parts of the

Wendy Madsen (left), special projects manager, and author Linda Graves Fabian inspect early demolition of the interior of the Wyoming Capitol during renovation from 2017 to 2019. *Starley Talbott photograph.*

capitol did not adhere to standards set by the Americans with Disabilities Act. The entire electrical system was obsolete, and plumbing and heating systems were badly corroded. Some stones had been damaged, paint was peeling, and corrosion was found in many areas of the exterior of the building.

The capitol's rehabilitation included the reorganization of all mechanical, electrical and plumbing systems to be located in vertical chases from the garden level through the attic. Two new elevators and interior staircases were added. Restrooms were added on every floor on both the east and west wings of the building (prior to renovation, there was only one public restroom, located on the garden level).

Some elements in the capitol have changed only slightly over the years. The checkerboard marble floors are one of its most notable features. The white marble is Italian. The black squares are called Swanton black and came from a quarry in Vermont. Near the top of the east stairs, one of the spindles was installed upside down; it is said that the carpenters who

The first phase of the Wyoming Capitol, around 1888. *Wyoming State Archives, Department of State Parks and Cultural Resources.*

The Wyoming Capitol several years after the first and second additions had been added to the building, around the 1930s. *J.E. Stimson Collection, Wyoming State Archives, Department of State Parks and Cultural Resources.*

installed the woodwork placed it upside down to remind folks that only God is perfect. The elegant staircases, like most of the woodwork throughout the capitol, are made of cherry imported by rail from Sandusky, Ohio. The woodwork has been refurbished and restored to its original sheen.

Legislators expressed a desire for increased public meeting space, so there will be four public meeting rooms in the capitol, with two on the first floor seating 45 people, a third-floor meeting room seating 45 and a restored Territorial Chamber that will seat 70 people. The Capitol Square Complex renovation also added six public meeting rooms in the Capitol Extension (a reconfiguration of the underground passageway from the capitol to the Herschler Office Building). Space for a 250-seat auditorium was also set aside for future renovations.

During demolition to repair various parts of the capitol, significant historical elements were discovered that had been altered or covered over during previous renovation projects. Previous work on the building had included the use of dropped ceilings to cover mechanical, electrical and plumbing systems. By moving those systems, the dropped ceilings were no longer necessary, and the monumental ceiling heights were restored. Previously hidden historic decorative elements, such as coffered ceilings, cornices, ornate columns, arched doorways, tall windows, decorative door knobs and woodwork have been restored to their original grandeur.

The exposure of windows that had been partly or totally obscured and the addition of skylights and lay lights throughout the building have flooded

An original brass door knob at the capitol had been covered over by a wall during previous renovation. It was discovered during the 2017–19 renovation. *Starley Talbott photograph.*

The decorative ceiling in the capitol rotunda has been returned to its original 1888 design. *Starley Talbott photograph.*

it with natural light. The east wall of the house chamber received the restoration of three historic windows that had been filled in during a 1970s project. All of the interiors of the capitol have been repainted with historic paint finishes, and the decorative ceiling in the rotunda was returned to its original 1888 design.

Art and architectural elements were originally integrated into the entire building following the neoclassical tradition. Statuary niches provided in the rotunda of the Wyoming Capitol had remained empty before the current renovation. The addition of four statues created by the sculptor Delissalde representing truth, courage, justice and hope will represent a timeless integration of art and architecture in style and content to the rotunda niches.

One of the most spectacular renovations is the restoration of the two-story grandeur of the historic Wyoming Territorial Assembly Chamber. The Wyoming Capitol earned its 1973 national historic landmark designation not for its architecture but for its historic importance in the history of women's suffrage. It was in this chamber that the territorial legislature approved the right of women to vote as an important feature of the initiative to form the state of Wyoming. The 1888 Territorial House Chamber was later occupied by the Wyoming Supreme Court and even later by the Legislative Services Office. The chamber was restored to its original size by eliminating a partition wall and reclaiming the two-story volume and public balcony. Original features were restored, including the stained-glass lay light and chandelier that had been located in Room 302. Artists from EverGreene Architectural Arts stenciled a decorative paint pattern on the ceiling of the historic chamber and added trompe l'oeil patterns to the walls. This magnificent room is now the largest meeting room in the capitol and will seat approximately seventy-five members of the public.

The 1888 territorial council (senate) was housed in the room that was most recently occupied by the Joint Appropriations Committee, on the second floor on the south side of the rotunda. The Legislative Services Office has been moved to this location, and the office is accessible to the public year-

Stenciling on the ceiling and restoration of the 1888 trompe l'oeil pattern on the walls was provided by EverGreene Architectural Arts in the historic Wyoming Territorial Assembly and Supreme Court Chamber. *Starley Talbott photograph.*

Craftsmen from EverGreene Architectural Arts observe progress at the Wyoming Capitol during the 2017–19 renovation. *Starley Talbott photograph.*

Michael Dixon, preservation architect, and author Starley Talbott review the renovation project while standing in the room where the 1888 territorial council met, now the location of the Legislative Services Office. *Linda Graves Fabian photograph.*

round. The doors into this room are open for the public to enjoy the view down Capitol Avenue to the historic train depot. The room also includes a small legislative research library.

Corridors on the north and south sides of the house and senate galleries have been restored to their historic configuration, and each gallery will be filled with natural light. Platform bench seating was removed from the galleries and theater seating was added to provide safer and more comfortable seating for the public. Public restrooms were also added to the house and senate third-floor lobbies.

Previous elevator locations outside the public galleries were difficult to navigate and did not meet ADA access standards. Elevators were moved to a different location. This provided an open corridor, allowing visual connection from the house gallery lobby to the senate gallery lobby.

The exterior of the capitol was updated, and some of the worn sandstone and masonry was replaced or repaired. The metal windows were replaced with wood windows designed to match the historic windows that had been removed in previous restorations.

The capitol dome was swathed in white sheet-like covering for months. The dome is constructed of copper gilded in gold leaf. Craftsmen from Renaissance Roofing Inc. replaced some of damaged parts of the dome before gilding. The dome panels were covered with gold leaf imported from

Laying the cornerstone of the Wyoming State Capitol on May 18, 1887. *Wyoming State Archives, Department of State Parks and Cultural Resources.*

Italy. A total of about seven ounces of gold was used in the gilding process. The gold-leaf dome of the capitol is an icon in Wyoming that sparkles with renewed glory for all of the state to celebrate.

Wyoming's thirty-second governor, Matt Mead, stated, "The restored Capitol will stand for the next century—a symbol of Wyoming statehood and all it encompasses. It will welcome visitors and those who participate in government. The Capitol is, perhaps, the most important building in the state. It represents the ideals of the people of Wyoming, now, just as it did when the cornerstone was laid 130 years ago."[69]

Notes

Introduction

1. Ewig, Rollins and Giffin, *Wyoming's Capitol*, 1.
2. Larson, *History of Wyoming*, 259.

Chapter 1

3. Ibid, 145.
4. Withey, Henry and Elsie, *Biographical Dictionary of American Architects*, 231.
5. Larson, *History of Wyoming*, 333.

Chapter 2

6. Ewig, "The Letters of John A. Feick," 2–14.
7. John Adam Feick III (great-grandson of John Adam Feick), e-mail message to author, June 18, 2018.

Chapter 3

8. Larson, *History of Wyoming*, 259–60.

9. "Speech by Theresa A. Jenkins," *Cheyenne Daily Leader*, July 24, 1890, and "Speech by Theresa A. Jenkins," *Cheyenne Daily Sun*, July 24, 1890.
10. Larson, *History of Wyoming*, 260.
11. *Wyoming Tribune-Eagle*, July 22, 1990.

Chapter 4

12. Larson, *History of Wyoming*, 122–26.
13. Jackson, "The Administration of Thomas Moonlight," 139–62.
14. Drake, "Francis E. Warren."
15. Larson, *History of Wyoming*, 448.
16. Van Pelt, "Big Nose George: A Grisly Frontier Tale."
17. Talbott, *Platte County*, 7, 25.
18. Larson, *History of Wyoming*, 447.
19. Georgen, "John B. Kendrick."
20. Carroll, "John B. Kendrick, Cowpoke to Senator," 51–57.
21. Larson, *History of Wyoming*, 448–49.
22. Rea, "The Ambition of Nellie Tayloe Ross."
23. Scheer, *Governor Lady*, 86.
24. Ibid., 87.
25. Ibid., 90.
26. Ibid., preface.
27. Ross, "The Governor Lady," 72–73, 180–95.
28. Wyoming State Archives, biography file, Nellie Tayloe Ross.
29. Larson, *History of Wyoming*, 460.
30. Shannon, "Fond Memories of Past Heads of State."
31. Larson, *History of Wyoming*, 463–67.
32. Ibid, 545.
33. Ibid, 548–51.
34. Ibid, 556–60.
35. Ibid, 560–67.
36. Ibid, 567–70.
37. Shannon, "Fond Memories of Past Heads of State."
38. Wyoming State Archives, biography file, Mike Sullivan.
39. Porter, "Mike Sullivan: 2016 Citizen of the West."
40. Brown, "Chat with a Hat."
41. Wyoming State Archives, biography file, Matt Mead.
42. Roberts, "Wyoming Becomes a State."

43. Larson, *History of Wyoming*, 256.
44. Wyoming Legislative Service Office.
45. Van Pelt, "William Jefferson Hardin."
46. Van Pelt, "Liz Byrd."
47. Wyoming Legislative Service Office.
48. Drake, "Estelle Reel."
49. Wyoming House of Representatives, House Bill No. HB0108 (2018).
50. Drake, "Thyra Thomson."
51. *Wyoming Tribune-Eagle*, "Obituary of Thyra Thomson," June 18, 2013.

Chapter 5

52. Wyoming State Historic Preservation Office, "National Register of Historic Places."
53. Ewig, "Did She Do That?," 26–34.
54. Larson, *History of Wyoming*, 92.
55. Docket of Esther Hobart Morris, Wyoming State Archives.
56. Massie, "Reform Is Where You Find It," 2–22.
57. Moulton, *Forts, Fights, and Frontier Sites*, 194–95.
58. "Chief Washakie's Obituary," 81.
59. Wyoming State Historic Preservation Office, "National Register of Historic Places."
60. Ward and Temple, *Elling William "Bill" Gollings*.
61. Gollings, "Autobiography of Elling William Gollings," 704–14.
62. Wyoming State Historic Preservation Office, "National Register of Historic Places."
63. True and Kirby, *Allen True: An American Artist*.
64. Wyoming State Archives.
65. Nickerson, "Riot at the 12th Wyoming Legislature."
66. *Wyoming State Tribune*, "Fisticuffs on the House Floor."

Chapter 6

67. Wyoming State Archives.

Chapter 7

68. Wendy Madsen, special projects manager, state of Wyoming, personal interviews with the authors, November 10, 2017, and April 17, 2018.
69. Girt, "Saving Wyoming's Architectural Treasure."

BIBLIOGRAPHY

Brown, Larry. "Chat with a Hat Reveals Sullivan's Story," *Casper Star-Tribune*, December 21, 1997.

Carroll, Eugene. "John B. Kendrick, Cowpoke to Senator 1879–1917." *Annals of Wyoming* 54, no. 1 (Spring 1982): 51–57.

Cheyenne Daily Leader. "Speech by Theresa A. Jenkins." July 24, 1890.

Cheyenne Daily Sun. "Joseph M. Carey Welcomed Home." July 27, 1890.

———. "Speech by Theresa A. Jenkins." July 24, 1890.

———. "Wyoming's Day." July 24, 1890.

"Chief Washakie's Obituary." *Wyoming Annals* 11, no. 1 (January 1939): 81.

Drake, Kerry. "Estelle Reel, First Woman Elected to Statewide Office in Wyoming." WyoHistory.org: A Project of the Wyoming State Historical Society. November 8, 2014. https://www.wyohistory.org/encyclopedia/estelle-reel.

———. "Francis E. Warren: A Massachusetts Farm Boy Who Changed Wyoming," WyoHistory.org: A Project of the Wyoming State Historical Society. November 8, 2014. https://www.wyohistory.org/encyclopedia/francis-e-warren-massachusetts-farm-boy-who-changed-wyoming.

———. "Thyra Thomson, a Secretary of State Worth Remembering." WyoFile: People, Places & Policy. June 25, 2013. https://www.wyofile.com/thyra-thomson-a-secretary-of-state-worth-remembering/.

Ewig, Rick. "Did She Do That? Examining Esther Morris' Role in the Passage of the Suffrage Act." *Annals of Wyoming* 78, no. 1 (Winter 2006): 26–34.

————. "The Letters of John A. Feick," *Annals of Wyoming* 59, no. 1 (Spring 1987): 2–14.

Ewig, Rick, Linda Rollins and Betty Giffin. *Wyoming's Capitol.* Cheyenne: Wyoming State Press, 1987.

Feick, Anita Gundlach. *Building America: A History of the Family Feick.* Baltimore: Gateway Press, 1983.

Feick, John Adam, and Feick Brothers. Letters. Wyoming State Archives.

Georgen, Cynde. "John B. Kendrick: Cowboy, Cattle King, Governor and U.S. Senator." WyoHistory.org: A Project of the Wyoming State Historical Society. November 8, 2014. https://www.wyohistory.org/encyclopedia/john-kendrick.

Girt, Rachel. "Saving Wyoming's Architectural Treasure for Future Generations." *Wyoming Rural Electric News,* July 2017.

Gollings, E.W. "Autobiography of Elling William Gollings, the Cowboy Artist." *Annals of Wyoming* 9, no. 2 (October 1932): 704–14.

Hobart Morris, Esther. Docket. Wyoming State Archives.

Jackson, W. Turrentine. "The Administration of Thomas Moonlight," *Annals of Wyoming* 18, no. 2 (July 1946): 139–62.

Larson, T.A. *History of Wyoming.* Lincoln: University of Nebraska Press, 1965.

Massie, Michael A. "Reform Is Where You Find It: The Roots of Woman Suffrage in Wyoming." *Annals of Wyoming* 62, no. 1 (Spring 1990): 2–22.

Moulton, Candy. *Forts, Fights, and Frontier Sites.* Glendo, WY: High Plains Press, 2010.

————. *Roadside History of Wyoming.* Missoula, MT: Mountain Press Publishing Company, 1995.

Nickerson, Gregory. "Riot at the 12th Wyoming Legislature: Fisticuffs on the House Floor." WyoHistory.org: A Project of the Wyoming State Historical Society. May 24, 2015. https://www.wyohistory.org/encyclopedia/riot-12th-wyoming-legislature-fisticuffs-house-floor.

Peeke, Hewson L. *A Standard History of Erie County, Ohio.* Chicago: Lewis Publishing, 1916.

Porter, William. "Mike Sullivan: 2016 Citizen of the West." *Denver Post,* January 6, 2016.

Rea, Tom. "The Ambition of Nellie Tayloe Ross." WyoHistory.org: A Project of the Wyoming State Historical Society. November 8, 2014. https://www.wyohistory.org/encyclopedia/ambition-nellie-tayloe-ross.

————. "John Campbell and the Invention of Wyoming." WyoHistory.org: A Project of the Wyoming State Historical Society. April 15,

2015. https://www.wyohistory.org/encyclopedia/john-campbell-and-invention-wyoming.

———. "Right Choice, Wrong Reasons: Wyoming Women Win the Right to Vote." WyoHistory.org: A Project of the Wyoming State Historical Society. November 8, 2014. https://www.wyohistory.org/encyclopedia/right-choice-wrong-reasons-wyoming-women-win-right-vote.

Roberts, Phil. "Wyoming Becomes a State: The Constitutional Convention and the Statehood Debates of 1889 and 1890—and Their Aftermath." WyoHistory.org: A Project of the Wyoming State Historical Society. November 8, 2014. https://www.wyohistory.org/encyclopedia/wyoming-statehood.

Ross, Nellie Tayloe. "The Governor Lady." *Good Housekeeping*, October 1927.

Scheer, Teva J. *Governor Lady: The Life and Times of Nellie Tayloe Ross*. Columbia: University of Missouri Press, 2005.

Shannon, Mary. "Fond Memories of Past Heads of State Are Shared," *Wyoming State Tribune*, Centennial Edition, July 1990.

Talbott, Starley. *Platte County*. Charleston, SC: Arcadia Publishing, 2009.

True, Jere, and Victoria Tupper Kirby. *Allen True: An American Artist*. San Francisco: Canyon Leap, in association with the Museum of the Rockies, Montana State University, Bozeman, 2009.

Van Pelt, Lori. "Big Nose George: A Grisly Frontier Tale." WyoHistory. org: A Project of the Wyoming State Historical Society. November 15, 2014. https://www.wyohistory.org/encyclopedia/big-nose-george-grisly-frontier-tale.

———. *Capital Characters of Old Cheyenne*. Glendo, WY: High Plains Press, 2006.

———. "Liz Byrd, First Black Woman in Wyoming's Legislature." Wyoming State Historical Society. May 24, 2015. https://www.wyohistory.org/encyclopedia/liz-byrd-first-black-woman-wyoming-legislature.

———. "William Jefferson Hardin: Wyoming's First Black Legislator." Wyoming State Historical Society. November 8, 2014. https://www.wyohistory.org/encyclopedia/william-jefferson-hardin.

Ward, William T., and Gary L. Temple. *Elling William "Bill" Gollings: A Cowboy Artist (1878–1932)*. Saratoga, WY: Patagonia Publishing Company, 2007.

Withey, Henry and Elsie. *Biographical Dictionary of American Architects*. Los Angeles: New Age Publishing Company, 1956.

Wyoming Legislative Service Office.

Wyoming State Historic Preservation Office. "National Register of Historic Places Inventory—Nomination Form," 1973.

Wyoming State Tribune. "Fisticuffs on the House Floor," January 20, 1913.
———. "Nellie Tayloe Ross Becomes Wyoming's Governor at Noon Monday with Simple Ceremony." January 5, 1925.
Wyoming Tribune-Eagle. "Obituary of Thyra Thompson." June 18, 2013.
———. "Tuesday's Event to Feature Statehood Parade, It's the Parade of the Century," July 22, 1990.

Websites

WyoHistory.org: A Project of the Wyoming State Historical Society. wyohistory.org.
Wyoming Capitol Square Project. wyomingcapitolsquare.com.
Wyoming Newspapers: From the Wyoming State Library. newspapers.wyo.gov.
Wyoming State Archives. wyoarchives.state.wy.us.
Wyoming State Historic Preservation Office. wyoshpo.state.wy.us.

ABOUT THE AUTHORS

Starley Talbott has been a freelance author for more than forty years. She has been published in numerous newspapers and magazines throughout the Rocky Mountain region and is the author of seven books, including three Arcadia Publishing titles: *Platte County*, *Fort Laramie* and *Cheyenne Frontier Days*; and one History Press title: *Wyoming Airmail Pioneers*. Starley holds a bachelor of science degree from the University of Wyoming and a master of science degree from the University of Nevada. She has lived in several states and foreign countries, loves to travel and has a deep appreciation for history. She is a member of Wyoming Writers, Platte County Historical Society and the Wyoming State Historical Society.

Linda Graves Fabian is the executive secretary of the Wyoming State Historical Society, a nonprofit, membership-driven organization with headquarters in Wheatland, Wyoming. She was previously employed for twenty years at the Wyoming Department of State Parks & Cultural Resources, where she served as the chief public information officer and the State History Day co-coordinator. A Wyoming native, Linda has a deep appreciation for the history of Wyoming and its people. She is the coauthor of two Arcadia Publishing titles: *Douglas* and *Cheyenne Frontier Days*. Linda is a member of the Platte County Historical Society and the Wyoming State Historical Society.